Grammar
for a
FULL
LIFE

How the Ways We Shape
a Sentence Can Limit
or Enlarge Us

Lawrence Weinstein

Grammar for a Full Life
How the Ways We Shape a Sentence Can Limit or Enlarge Us
Lawrence Weinstein

LEXIGRAPHIC
PUBLISHING

Published by Lexigraphic Publishing, Cambridge, Massachusetts

Cover Design: Ayman Alalao
Interior Design and Layout: Marie Stirk

Cover Illustration and Drawings on pages 54, 71, 149, 156, and 189: Juliana Duclos

Publisher's Cataloging-In-Publication Data
(Prepared by The Donohue Group, Inc.)

Names: Weinstein, Larry, 1948- author.
Title: Grammar for a full life : how the ways we shape a sentence can limit
    or enlarge us / Lawrence Weinstein.
Description: Cambridge, MA : Lexigraphic Publishing, [2020] | Includes
    bibliographical references and index.
Identifiers: ISBN 9781734692709 (paperback) | ISBN 9781734692716 (ePub)
    | ISBN 9781734692723 (Kindle)
Subjects: LCSH: English language—Grammar—Psychological aspects. |
    Expression (Philosophy)
Classification: LCC PE1398.P79 W45 2020 (print) | LCC PE1398.P79 (ebook)
    | DDC 425.9—dc23

To tell how near a soul has come to being fully realized, the sign is speech.

— Nachman of Bratzlav

Contents

To Diane's memory . . . and the live Suzanne.

Introduction

The limits of my language mean the limits of my world.

— LUDWIG WITTGENSTEIN

When my devoted wife, Diane Weinstein, was still living—and avidly contributing her input on the first version of this book—I had a cockeyed dream one night in which she played a crucial part.

In that dream, dinner guests of ours were going for their coats and readying to leave when Diane suddenly came out of the kitchen holding an oversized pot by two handles and chiding me, saying, "You forgot to serve the alphabet soup."

At these words, I turned red, sensing the enormity of my omission. I dutifully corralled a few bewildered guests back to our dinner table.

Those few sat right down, picked up spoons, and stared for a moment at what lay in front of them: an engrossing mix of letters and punctuation marks circulating freely in their bowls. They used their spoons to have some wary sips of the dish.

will also somewhat *mold* their thinking. Whorf argued that, by making certain thoughts easier to express than others, a language helps determine what one thinks and feels in the first place. In English, for example, we have tenses that separate the present from the past—that put the past behind us, in effect, implying it will never come again—and most of us who *think* in English therefore try not to "waste" time; we move frenziedly. By comparison, the Hopi Indians Whorf studied, whose management of tense implied that "everything that ever happened still is," had less anxiety than most of us do and led more measured lives. A language, Whorf believed, can contribute either to neuroses (his term) or to more expansive, adaptive ways of thinking and being.

I asked myself, Could the same be said of each of the distinctive tongues I had been hearing *within* English? Could the variations from one English speaker to the next be linked to different ways of thinking and living, not all of which are equally likely to foster well-being? If so, that seemed to be worth knowing, since making some few tweaks to one's persistent set of grammar practices might, then, alter one's time spent on Earth in consequential ways.

It was at that point in my thinking, though, when my train-of-thought temporarily derailed—and a good thing, too. I soon learned that Whorf had many detractors in the field of linguistics. More importantly, I soon had to concede that their critiques were largely valid ones, based on evidence. In particular, I saw that most of the effects Whorf attributed to vocabulary and/or grammar can't, in fact, be produced through language *per se*, language not reinforced by cultural or other factors.

thoughtless wailing except to surmise that, in our species' long past, infants whose DNA predisposed them to endure pain and hunger in silence didn't generally survive long enough to pass their mutant, quiet gene along to offspring of their own? Unfortunately, though, my simply making noise—or uttering full sentences, as an adult—doesn't always do the trick of winning others' ears. In settings where it doesn't, I feel as if I'm talking to the wall, and my confidence sometimes deserts me, leaving me to doubt I have as much a right to speak as others present do.

Which brings me to the colon.

The biologist/essayist Lewis Thomas found colons—those two vertically arranged dots that say, "Listen up, please. Here's what you should know"—"a lot less attractive" than semicolons. "Firstly," he writes, "they give you the feeling of . . . having your nose pointed in a direction you might not be inclined to take if left to yourself."

On the other hand, Strunk and White, the renowned authors of *The Elements of Style*, don't seem to have shared Thomas's aversion. In their own book, sometimes they employ a colon to oblige us to study and absorb a model of correctness, as in

Punctuate as follows: Wednesday, August 14, 1929.

Elsewhere, they use the colon to compel us to observe what can happen when a writer *disregards* one of their famous rules, an example being the colon at the end of

Sentences violating Rule 7 are often ludicrous:

Those two vertically arranged dots of a colon have much the same riveting effect as the two loud clinks on a piece of glassware that announce a wedding toast—or the two decisive taps of a baton that call an orchestra to order. (Or think back to the teacher you had in elementary school who, to get your boisterous class's attention, sometimes flicked the classroom lights off and on.)

As E. B. White (the White of "Strunk and White") tells it, William Strunk "felt it was worse to be irresolute than to be wrong." He had been White's teacher in college, and one day in class he had "leaned far forward, in . . . the pose of a man about to impart a secret—and croaked, 'If you don't know how to pronounce a word, say it loud!'" Strunk's use of colons—like so much else in *The Elements of Style*—bares the unapologetic self at the top of its form. It says, "I have standing in this place, so heed me."

Which way to punctuate, then: that of the quietly respectful Lewis Thomas, or that of the assertive Strunk? Even if we somewhat prefer Thomas as a personality, can we always do without recourse to Strunk's in-your-face grammatical maneuvers?

I am here addressing people who would just as soon colonize a foreign nation as "colon-ize" a sentence. To them (and are you one of them?), that two-pointed mark is a double-barreled shotgun; they keep it locked away. They might stand across the counter from the most unhelpful clerk at a hotel, waiting overlong to check in with him and get their keys in time to make their niece's graduation, and still not feel at liberty to capture his attention with the filler sound and speech inflection that correspond to a written colon, as in,

> Uhh, hello there, sir. I have a complaint to lodge with you: For twenty minutes now . . . .

It's the spoken colon after "you" that lays claim to all the airtime needed to express the rest.

Back at home, my father used to say, "Don't let people walk all over you." In his business correspondence—with which, as a boy, I used to help him, since he was an immigrant who never fully mastered English usage—he would insert colons frequently. Each pair of dots was typographical fair warning to the reader (the customer who'd sent him three bouncing checks in a row, the boss who had spoiled some of his sales through ill-advised pricing decisions, etc.) that he'd better not ignore my father's next few words.

On a much larger stage, we have the example of a colon—or momentous, colon-like pause—which arrested the nation's attention at a march on Washington in August, 1963. The speaker, a 34-year-old black minister from Alabama, said, "I still have a dream" and boldly then deployed a remarkable colon (of the spoken kind) before spelling his dream out. It was his way of requesting that an audience of millions tune out everything but him for a moment; his forthcoming words were that important.

> I still have a dream:
>   . . . I have a dream that one day this nation will rise up and live out the true

> meaning of its creed: "We hold these truths
> to be self-evident: that all men are created
> equal."

Would he have succeeded in winning others' ears—and in being memorable—if he *hadn't* first, by pausing, implicitly announced his right to full attention? Let my reader be the judge. A colon-less alternative might have read as follows:

> I still have a dream that one day this nation
> will rise up and live out the true meaning of
> its creed . . . .

Though I am not as bold a soul as Martin Luther King, I retain the colon in my verbal repertoire, and I suggest that other meek or mild types do so, too. We must learn to insist that we have rights to airtime. Our increased use of that punctuation mark—written or spoken—is one fine way to begin.

Tapping Inborn Energy

Transitive Verbs in the Active Voice

Not long ago, I was sitting in a neighborhood café for breakfast when a four-year-old boy at the next table suddenly stopped blowing his food cool (which he had been doing with unreal intensity) and proclaimed, "I could eat the whole w-o-o-o-r-l-d today!"

He was going to do with pancakes—and then, apparently, with you and me and the entire planet we call home—just as he pleased.

I had to laugh. An electric rush went up my spine at his sublime declaration of power.

Truth to tell, I have sometimes found myself drawing on the same pool of naive energy, or felt-potentiality, that he was drawing on. At such moments I have also spoken brazenly, transitively (definition coming in the next page or two). Beginning at around age 4, I, like him, have always envisioned *doing* different things to the preexisting world—owning it (or a gorgeous piece of it), consuming it, rousing it from slumber and setting it straight (as with this book I'm writing) . . . and so forth.

Is that immature on my part? I suppose that in some light it is, but I wonder: Can the world's deeds be performed by people who no longer thrill internally at the prospect of having life their way?

Walt Disney was, in my opinion, hardly the only captain of industry—or benefactor of society—who went through all adulthood partly as a child. Every founder of a start-up (I mean people in the mold of Steve Jobs at Apple), every architect, every social reformer with a vision—even every owner of a house who plants a backyard garden—is a sibling of the man Walt Disney was when he set plans in motion to create Disneyland. He or she, like Disney, is internally a four-year-old who is going to bend the world to her inspired will. Her life story, too, is one of trying to revamp reality until it corresponds to the private dream of how things *should* be.

Freud's onetime disciple Alfred Adler had this animating, innate wish in mind by his phrase "the striving for perfection." Without it, Adler said, "life would be unthinkable."

And yet if, as we mature, we don't take sufficient verbal care, certain features of the grammar we adopt will drain us even of the modicum of energy it takes to have the oil in our car changed or to cast a ballot on Election Day. The roundabout linguistic moves I have in mind will rob us of our potency by depriving us of mental *pictures* of our bold, birthright selves.

That takes some explaining—including setting forth what are, for some, the hardest grammatical distinctions to master in this book. Please stay with me for just one or two pages about them.

Most verbs in English answer to one of these names:

- transitive verb in the active voice
- *intransitive* verb in the active voice, or
- transitive verb in the *passive* voice.

That's right: in that order, for my purposes in this chapter. What, to begin with, does "transitive" mean?

A *transitive* verb is a verb that takes an object. That is, when I use a transitive, I must name the thing or person sitting at that verb's receiving end, which it impacts. If I use the verb *washed* (in one of its transitive meanings), I must not stop there; I must move right on to say exactly what or who got cleaner. The sentence that results is, "With great difficulty, my Aunt Jenny washed the cat."

Not surprisingly, then, an *intransitive* verb is one that doesn't take an object. A good example is *arrived*. I can say, "My Aunt Jenny has arrived" but not "My Aunt Jenny has arrived the cat." She can spoil, wash, hate, or love the cat, but not arrive it.

In *passive* voice, we go back to transitive verbs, but we reverse the order of subject and object, so that whatever is *receiving* the action—the thing or person *impacted* by the action—comes first, taking center stage. Oddly enough, in passive voice, the performer of the action, such as diligent

Aunt Jenny, may not even get a fleeting mention. Frequently, the use of passive voice results in sentences like "The cat was being washed."

- **And so, if I say, "The boy devoured an imposing pile of syrup-heavy pancakes,"** I am speaking in the active voice, and the verb I'm using is a transitive verb. Because, in active voice, the performer of the action in my sentence—*The boy*—appears up front as the subject of my sentence, the mind turns out an image of him instantly. What is more, by virtue of my using a transitive verb there, *devoured*, the mind is rapidly supplied with a picture of *what* the boy eats: *syrup-heavy pancakes*. That combination of active voice and transitive verb is the most direct and vivid mode available to us for rendering an act in words. Just in rereading my sentence, I feel energized by it. While I was first writing it, it proved even more invigorating.

- **If instead I say, "That boy ate well,"** I am still in active voice (with the doer of the deed, the boy, still upfront, in subject position), but my strong transitive verb, *devoured*—and its direct object, *syrup-heavy pancakes*—have been supplanted by *ate*, which, as an *intransitive* verb (in its use here), has *no* direct object. The boy remains visible, but his food does not.

- **If finally I say, "Those pancakes were devoured,"** I have crossed the boundary out of active voice altogether and begun to speak in passive voice, where, incredibly, the verb's direct object, those enticing pancakes, takes the sentence over, usurping the position that would logically be thought to belong to the person whose act the sentence describes. It's as if *no* person (or even cat) were involved in the pancakes' disappearance.

What is, I think, crucial to note about my list of three verb types above is this: *that with each move away from the original active/transitive mode of expression, one's awareness of the proactive role played in the story by a fellow human being diminishes further.* Especially passive voice constructions like "Those pancakes were devoured"—which eliminate the doer of the deed from view (or tack him/her on as an afterthought, as in "devoured . . . by that boy")—tend to reinforce the misunderstanding that things "just happen."

Famously, government officials and others call upon the passive voice to avoid being held accountable for bad decisions they have made, but I'm leaving to another chapter my thoughts on the ethics of such shirking of responsibility.

At the moment, I want to consider an enormous cost of passivity in grammar that isn't much discussed: how, in representing the events of life as happening with no person at the helm, *choosing* to act, the passive voice robs us over time of our core sense of agency. When I read or hear such passive utterances—or, worse yet, generate such fatalistic language myself—it leaves me feeling powerless about the very situation being referenced in the words, since I get no picture of a member of my species *doing* something in relation to it.

For example, take this common circumstance: Someone finds herself on hold on the phone for longer than she bargained for when she first placed her call. A member of her household walks into the room where she's standing and asks her, "What's happening?" Her possible replies include

> **the passive** "I am being kept on hold," where the speaker, "I," is merely the recipient of an action being carried out by someone unnamed,

> **and the active** "I've been holding for ten minutes now."

Of these two responses, which is more liable to leave the caller virtually stuck in the situation she reports, and which is likelier to enable her to get out from under its grip and hang up, if that's what makes best sense?

To my ear, the speaker of the passive, first line—where the speaker is just being *acted upon*—isn't nearly as prepared to put the phone down and get on with her day as the speaker of the active, second line, who, by saying "I've been holding . . . ," ensures that she'll remain aware of her own power to terminate the call in question at whatever point she'd like to do so.

I want to live more energetically than the man who (in passive voice) complains, "I *was caught* in rush hour," when he could have honestly reported (with self-agency), "I *left the office too late* to avoid rush hour."

What follows is a positive example of active constructions from the business world. I was surprised to find it in my mailbox, in a quarterly report to shareholders from the manager of a mutual fund. Stocks were then plunging, and he might have sought cover behind "forces beyond his control," repeatedly calling on the passive voice for that purpose, as many of his counterparts in other firms did.

He first admits to having made poor decisions, then elaborates,

> Within finance, for example, I added to the fund's stakes in more of the brokerage-type names such as Citicorp and Merrill Lynch, and I de-emphasized conservative areas such as regional banks.

When I found that in my mail, I thought, "How refreshing, in its quiet way!" Encountering the active voice in unadorned, straightforward phrases like *I added, I de-emphasized*—I felt incrementally empowered myself. This man was not, in the unseasoned manner of a preschooler eyeing pancakes, roaring, "Bring it on!" But neither was he buckling or trying just to blend into the wallpaper. He was gladly in the thick of life still. I told myself, "As a member of the same species to which this fund manager belongs, I must also have it in me to take action despite setbacks and the ongoing risks in my world." To my mind, the shareholder report was the embodiment of our imperfect, can-do America at its grammatical best. I almost didn't mind that its gist was that now I had less money for retirement than I'd thought I had.

For a last case here, I turn to psychologists Albert Ellis and Robert A. Harper, who actually propose a therapeutic use of transitive-active grammar. They counsel readers away from intransitive sentences like "My parents were the source of all my troubles and still are." That sort of sentence, they say,

> serves as a cop-out for your past and present behavior. If you acknowledge, instead, "My parents kept criticizing me severely during my childhood, and I kept taking them too seriously and thereby kept upsetting myself . . . ," you strongly imply what you can do to interrupt and change your own self-downing tendencies.

We are not mere victims. Within certain, quite important limits, we remain the makers of our fate.

Some sad grammatical constructions lead us to forget that fact—and so drain us of the juices indispensable for action. Others, however, keep that fact of life alive to consciousness, so that we are able to reshape the world anew from day to day, with at least some traces of a four-year-old's gusto.

The Wherewithal

Certain Prepositions

Here go four sentences in which, to varying degrees, the speaker can be seen to be in awe of someone else:

Unlike me, whose eyes become two helpless streams in flood near a sliced onion (making it impossible to see what I'm doing when I cook), Chef Omar on TV cuts onions without shedding a tear.

Even diving from our high board, Jamelle hits the pool splashlessly.

Detective Papazian can usually identify a photo that's been doctored, even if it looks genuine to everyone else.

The Ferolds made people of all colors, backgrounds, and personality types feel welcome at their home.

Though each of these sentences employs a transitive verb in the active voice—*cuts, hits, can identify, made*—each one stops short of naming the means by which its action is accomplished. It's as if each sentence opened with that question-begging adverb *somehow*. Somehow, Chef Omar keeps from crying while cutting onions. Somehow, Jamelle dives into pools without displacing water . . . .

Sentences like these call to mind the drawings turned out by four-year-olds in which people are missing one or more of the limbs actually required to perform the deeds pictured. The young artist may inform us that he's drawn a man flying a kite, but all that we are shown is an armless figure and a sort of trapezoidal shape above him in the sky—no string, no body part suitable for holding string. In its blindness to how the deed is done, such a drawing suggests that the artist is simply in awe; the idea that he himself could achieve a result like the one he depicts—an airborne kite—is inconceivable to him.

Yes, energy—the kind of energy suffusing active, transitive verbs—is essential to a life of "getting things done." It's not *all* that's called for, though. Agency demands an eye for means.

In the realm of children's art, a sense of agency demands (eventually) visualizing upper limbs with hands. In writing, as in speaking, it demands adding the *language of instrumentality*. It demands adding either whole sentences devoted to the "how of it" or, short of that, such elements of grammar as prepositional how-to phrases. The latter all begin with a preposition like *by, in, through,* or *from* and then go on to name the takeable steps (together with available devices) that make a feat conceivable, as in

Chef Omar manages to cut onions without shedding a tear **by** breathing only **through** his mouth **for** the duration.

or

Through a close study of the *shadows* made by objects in a photo—and **through** a careful reckoning of whether every shadow is consistent with the others—Detective Papazian can usually identify a photo that's been doctored.

Don't such phrases, which begin to break an operation down into its hidden parts, move that operation into closer range of our own ability?

We can empower ourselves by adding limb-like instrumental phrases to our speech and writing when reporting deeds worthy to be imitated. Any sentence that has done no more about an act than to name it is a mere torso, not a full assurance of our wherewithal to undertake such acts ourselves when the time comes.

Let's get specific, then. Circumstance will sometimes call for the insertion of a comma that the comma rules do not envision. We were taught to use commas to separate items in a series only when that series has at least three items in it, but that rule serves poorly in some cases. The following sentence adheres to that rule:

> Wallace Stevens wrote memos on questions
> of the insurance business and poetry.

Since the series in the sentence consists of only two items, "memos on questions of the insurance business" and "poetry," no comma comes between them. But the writer of the sentence meant the word *memos* to go only with *questions of the insurance business*—not that and *poetry*. Without a comma there, the sentence can be read to mean that poet Wallace Stevens's contribution to the world of poetry took the form of memos about it! (And reversing the order of the items hardly improves matters. Try it. The result is a sentence that can be read to mean Stevens's poetry dealt with issues in the insurance industry.) For communication's sake, we need

> Wallace Stevens wrote memos on questions
> of the insurance business, and poetry.

Or take the short sentence below. With the assistance of a comma that cannot be found in grammar books, it works perfectly—and without that impish comma, it wouldn't work at all.

> Nurses who can, retire from their jobs at
> age 62.

At times, such commas can even be justified on purely stylistic grounds. In the next sentence, Alice Walker ingeniously employs an unmandated comma for special effect:

> White men and women continued to run
> things, badly.

The comma carves out *two* end-positions for the statement (therefore, two points of emphasis) where otherwise there would be just one. If Walker wrote that sentence at a laptop, she probably had to ignore some automatic highlighting meant to correct her.

I propose a medical-sounding adjective for those who, unlike Walker, insert commas strictly by the rules, thoughtlessly, with no attention to the real effect they're having: *commatose*. But, in fact, the comma rules are not the only rules of grammar that a human being endowed with agency will break now and then. Scholars Margaret M. Bryant and Janet Rankin Aiken, writing sixty years ago in their book *Psychology of English*, rushed to the defense of a writer who violated the rule that singular subjects go with singular verbs, plural subjects with plural verbs:

> In saying "The tumult and the shouting dies"
> [rather than "die"], Kipling was utilizing the
> same instinct which would lead a formal man
> to select a matching tie and handkerchief.

Their implication—I agree with it—is that the words *tumult* and *shouting* may be separate and distinct, but *tumult and shouting* is a single phenomenon. As they later say,

> Only the myopia of scholarship can lead the grammarian to attempt to put grammar into a pigeonhole separate from living.

We must be at liberty to do what works.

While I'm at it, let me put a word in for sentences that are not complete. Yes, fragments.

"Yes, fragments" is, of course, itself a fragment. Did it confuse you? If not, did it fleetingly distract you, though? No? (There's *another* fragment.) Writing situations differ as to how much use of fragments will unofficially be countenanced, but one should push the envelope when they are what the situation calls for, in terms of conciseness or impact.

Revisiting the case of the defective traffic light, I readily concede that the worst, most lethal driver is the one who has no basis for knowing that the light's not working but obliviously runs it without waiting to find out. He probably runs *functioning* red lights, too, when he's in a hurry. By no means do I condone his disregard of one of the most vital rules of the road.

At the other far extreme, however, is the driver so cowed by authority that he not only sits frozen at his wheel for an eternity, crawling out into the intersection only after others have begun to pass him on the left, but, at that, feels deep resentment toward those other drivers for their lawlessness. If I'm right about him, he has never set to paper a paragraph consisting of just one sentence or started any sentence with the conjunction *or* (let alone coined a new word). His sense of agency in life could benefit from practicing transgression of just that magnitude and kind.

Pressed for Time

The Imperative

Another rule that we must learn to ignore occasionally is the wise rule of etiquette against issuing orders to other people.

If an electrician is working on a light switch in our front hallway when the front doorbell rings, it is that rule which keeps us from saying, "Get the door, Mr. Shay." Either we ourselves make our way to the door to see who's there or we resort to less direct syntactical forms, such as questions. We say, "Mr. Shay, would you mind getting that for me?"

But sometimes we need to cut to the chase.

Even in relationships based on strong mutual respect, occasions arise that call for shutting down the respectful instincts and shifting gears grammatically. They require the imperative mode of speech, in which the main clause starts with a verb, and the unnamed subject of that verb (the person we are wanting to "perform" the verb, so to speak) is always the person we're addressing. If, coming down the stairs on moving day, we start losing control of a heavy sofa, we call out to someone, in the imperative, "Give me a hand here, please!" (notice how the subject, "you," goes without saying) or just "Help!"

Or take the example of an emergency. If a woman has collapsed in a busy department store, someone needs to cry out, "Stand back! Stand back! Call 9-1-1, somebody!"

I, like you, have known "comfortable shouters." They don't need the encouragement contained in this chapter. They would find this chapter tame and should skip the rest of it.

That said, however, the imperative—that brashest of modes—represents a temperamental *stretch* for many of us— even for some of us whose jobs necessitate *preparedness* to use it, like the copilots of commercial jetliners. In the story behind one fatal plane crash, there was snow falling while the plane awaited clearance for takeoff. Ice was rapidly accumulating on the plane's wings, making them too heavy for flight. Freezing was occurring too fast for the airline's de-icing crew to keep up with it.

The "black box" recording of exchanges between pilot and copilot in those moments makes clear that the copilot under-stood the situation and was alarmed by it but had trouble using imperative grammar with his superior to convey urgency. He might have said, in the imperative, "Al, don't take off," but he didn't. Instead, what he said (in the normal, declarative mode) was

> Boy, this is a, this is a losing battle here on
> trying to de-ice those things. It [gives] you a
> false feeling of security, that's all that does.

Tragically, the recording ends thirty-seven seconds after takeoff, as follows:

> Copilot: Al, we're going down, Al.
> Captain: I know.

Admittedly, an extreme story—but everyone's life includes emergencies of some size, and these call for there to be a person on the scene ready to employ imperative language. How can someone—in particular, a quiet soul, for whom the shouted order is anathema—get in shape for taking charge at the inevitable moments in life when he or she or fellow human beings fall into harm's way?

Maybe she can start with emergencies that take days, rather than mere seconds, to play themselves out. And, in those cases, maybe she can start by shouting on paper, rather than aloud, since writing affords the would-be exclaimer a chance to get used to the sight of an exclamation mark before committing to it—a chance, that is, to *lower by degrees* her too-high barrier to shouting.

She can start with notes to a spouse that read, "Don't forget the cottage deposit!" or, "Tell the kids no diving!" She can go from there to honking when a car coming toward her on a dark road at night has no lights on. After she has gotten her writing hand moving in the imperative mode— and, perhaps, hit her car horn once or twice—all that's left to activate is her vocal cords.

The imperative doesn't have to be imperious. The four-year-old who's never gone swimming before may have trouble believing that a substance with as much loose play in it as water can hold him up. (I still marvel at the fact myself.) At such times, only doing can settle the question. We don't tell that child all the science involved; we say gently, but in the imperative, "Give it a try, you'll see" . . . and, of course, "I'll be right here to catch you if anything goes wrong."

The other times that warrant using the quiet imperative are those when enough is enough. We can't afford to let every last thing drag on in the effort to get it just right. One must, for example, occasionally say, imperatively, "Friends, we've been arguing for ten minutes about how to split the dinner bill. I can't speak for you, but I have better things to do with my evening. Here's a twenty-dollar bill to cover me. Gabi, Sal, you put in the same. Abigail, make yours eight and we'll be set." Unless (a) the amounts proposed stray grossly from the mark of equity or (b) someone at the table suffers from a personality disorder (in which case, of course, more care must be taken), the entire group is likely to feel grateful, even to laugh as they pull out their wallets.

People know that some allowance must be made for the shortness of life.

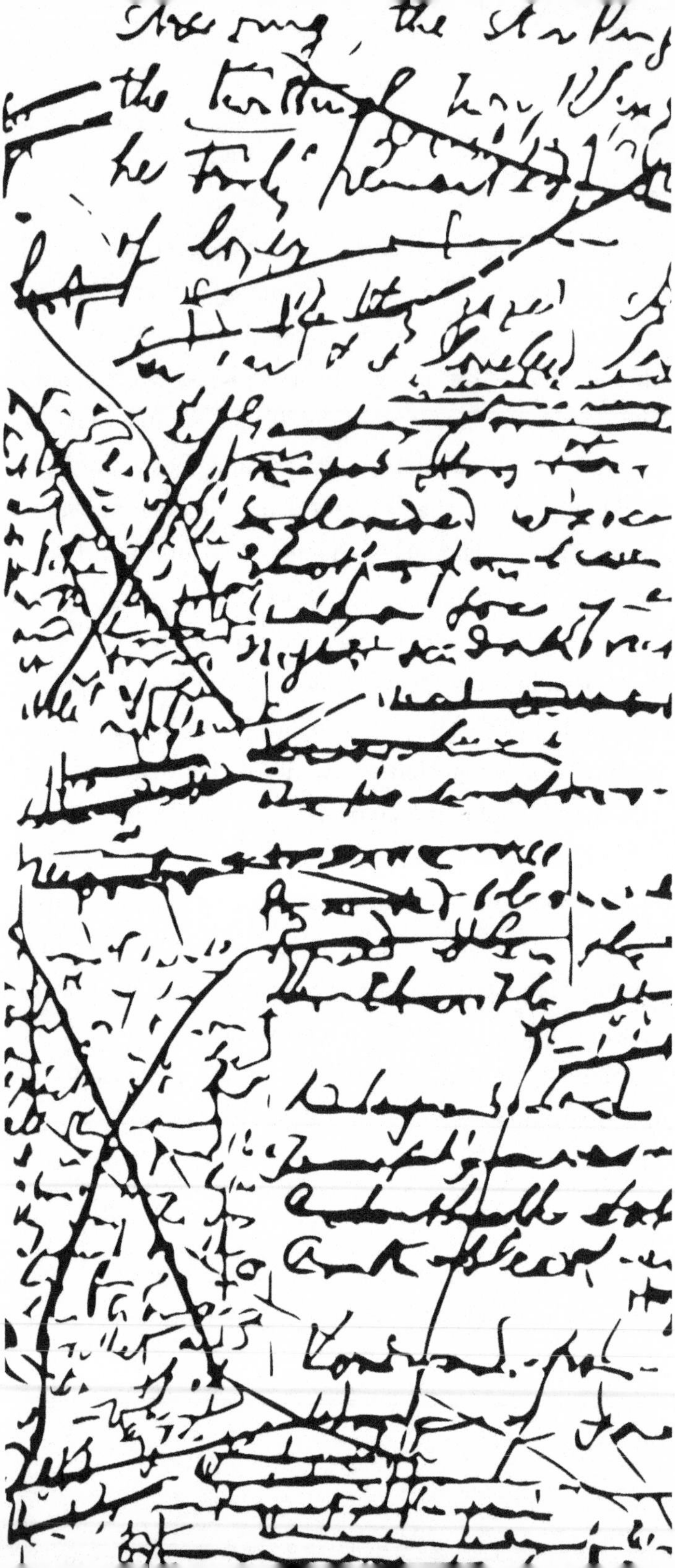

Section of a manuscript page by James Joyce

"No Effort Without Error"

Cross-Outs

Ernest Hemingway: I rewrote the ending to A Farewell to Arms, *the last page of it, thirty-nine times before I was satisfied.*

Interviewer: Was there some technical problem there? What was it that had you stumped?

Hemingway: Getting the words right.

. . . .

Getting it wrong is part of getting it right.
— CHARLES HANDY

No mark a writer puts to paper has more value than the one readers never get to see: the cross-out.

As a staunch believer in what I've just said, I was taken by the tone of surprise I thought I heard in yourself go wrong an unlimited number of times in a place where no one is watching: the terrain of paper, pens, and keyboards, *in your drafting phase*. When you next sit down to write an application essay, memo, letter to the editor, poem, or set of instructions for the babysitter, don't fear getting it wrong. Just aim for honesty, clarity, and impact. Nobody I know satisfies all three criteria right off the bat, except with shopping lists. It takes revising.

. . . As soon as you have come to see the need to cut or change some words, pause to give yourself a heartfelt (preferably audible) cheer. That very realization is proof of your capacity for doing this world's work.

When I edit my own writing, I still use an "X" to mark the false starts I will be discarding. Do you do the same? If it helps, think of both diagonally placed straight lines that comprise the "X" as slanted lines of text. Read the first line of the two (that would be the one from upper right to lower left, in my case) as proclaiming, *"an honorable stab at what is needed,"* and read the other line, canceling the first, as declaring, *"not there yet."* Each "X" on the page is then a badge of meritorious service to oneself and others (one's readers).

Tally the cross-outs. Do they come to but a measly one or two? Bad sign. Pull for many more the next time. (I'm not joking.)

I like the novelist Kurt Vonnegut's way of phrasing my point here:

> Novelists . . . have, on the average, about the same IQ as the cosmetic consultants at Bloomingdale's department store. Our power

is patience. We have discovered that writing allows even a stupid person to seem halfway intelligent, if only that person will write the same thought over and over again, improving it just a little bit each time. It is a lot like inflating a blimp with a bicycle pump. Anybody can do it. All it takes is time.

A satisfying finished piece of writing is but one good outcome of engagement in a full-blown process of revision at the writing table. Ideally, the other is more readiness to play a part in *all* types of effort requiring error-making.

I save for last the words of a lusty maker-of-mistakes—and at times, therefore, maker of real progress—Teddy Roosevelt. (I've replaced his now-dated use of "man" with other phraseology, to reflect us all.)

It is not the critic who counts; not the one who points out how the strong soul stumbles, or where the doer of deeds could have done them better. The credit belongs to the person who is actually in the arena, whose face is marred by dust and sweat and blood; who strives valiantly; who errs, who comes up short again and again, because there is no effort without error and shortcoming . . . .

GRAMMAR FOR
CREATIVE PASSIVITY

The right shot at the right moment does not come, because you do not let go of yourself . . . . *What stands in your way is that you have a much too willful will. You think that what you do not do for yourself does not happen.*

— JAPANESE ZEN
MASTER KENZO
AWA, QUOTED BY
EUGEN HERRIGEL IN
*ZEN IN THE ART OF
ARCHERY*

Having devoted the preceding section of this book to the theme of agency, I must issue an important caveat.

Agency, the felt capacity to make things happen, is, yes, indispensable in life. But, then, all too often, agency leads people who possess it to adopt a quite misleading anthem in their heads: "Resolve is all I need for doing what I wish to; I have only just to set my mind to my new goal and then apply myself."

That goes too far. We can get things done in life, but doing so requires joining agency with its essential opposite, receptivity.

When I was in eighth grade, the teacher who directed our boys glee club became so vexed by the effect my voice was having on her listening pleasure that one day she asked me to please just mouth the words silently from then on. Even at that age, I was sharp enough to take a hint and dropped out.

But I love to sing. I wish that she had taught me to relax my vocal cords, not prompted me to pack them up and take them home with me. In retrospect, I'm sure my sonic disruption of the glee club's performances stemmed from conscientiousness. It was my exertion of my throat's resources that prevented resonance and resulted in audible wear and tear.

Not until I was fifty did I try to pick up where I'd left off as a singer at fourteen. This time, though, I was lucky to find a teacher who could see my problem for what it was—lack of passivity—and prescribe for it accordingly. She told me that, when singing, I should imagine all the words and notes of a song crowding just behind my throat's opening, jostling each other as they press for their escape into the air. I would never need to force them out; they would fly out on their own instantly, if and when I gave them passage. I was nothing but their gatekeeper.

That's made all the difference.

In singing—and in most pursuits—we must add to agency a degree of relaxation. Without it, we get stiff and close off access to resources of the unconscious, such as those that regulate the vocal cords and airflow.

A person who, in speaking and/or writing, avoids the passive voice at all times, may be missing out on our best way to cultivate that mix of active/passive modes which produces many of the outcomes we long for in life.

In his quote on page 44, the recognized Zen master Kenzo Awa doesn't question our deep need to have a live, operative will (how else could I have made it to a local music school and discovered *the teacher who finally helped me?), but he does oppose a "too willful will."*

Getting Out of One's Own Way

Passive Voice

A relative of William James once tried to explain passive voice to a small girl. (Please note my italics in the next paragraph.)

"Suppose that *you* . . . kill *me*," said the grown-up. "You who *do* the killing are in the active voice, and I, who *have been killed*, am in the passive voice."

That smart girl wasn't satisfied, however.

How, she retorted, could a person even speak to *say*, in passive voice, "I've been killed," if, in fact, he *had* been killed?

"Well," said the faltering adult, "you must suppose I'm not quite dead yet."

The very next day, according to James, the child was put on the spot in class to explain the passive voice and said, "It's the kind of voice you speak in when you're not quite dead."

The theme of most commentary on the passive voice in our times appears to be its sad unfitness for use by writers who are not yet on their deathbeds.

Strunk and White lead the way. In *The Elements of Style* they proclaim—simply but resoundingly, as their Rule Number 10—"Use the active voice," and they press the case for "direct," "forcible" language. They don't favor the elimination of all passives; they themselves use the passive construction "can be made lively" on the same page. But their thrust is clear: to promote more writing like their own, which in general *has* straightforward thrust. (My earlier essay on the active voice, "Tapping Inborn Energy," also encourages this direct style of writing, when the occasion demands.)

Among the many strenuous opponents of the passive voice, a majority—taking their cue from George Orwell, in his essay "Politics and the English Language"—stress how easily that voice can be used to conceal accountability, since it doesn't call for the person or entity that performs the action of the verb to be named. The passive sentence "The dog hasn't been walked yet" stops well short of implicating any member of the household as the negligent appointed walker.

One can spot such concealment of responsibility—or, in the lesser case, downplaying of responsibility—in much of the language issued by government offices. It sounds like this:

> A secret shipment of arms to the insur-
> gents was requested on March 19, approved
> on March 20, and carried out on March 21.
> [*That's at least three different people who owe
> their anonymity to the passive voice.*]

Undeniably, mistakes were made. [*Yes, but who made them?*]

In the world of medicine, concealment of agency can sound like the following excerpt from a note a surgeon composed in 1961 at the request of comedian Lenny Bruce, for use in the event the heroin needle marks on his arms were noticed by police.

> Mr. Bruce suffers from episodes of severe depression and lethargy . . . . He has therefore been instructed in the proper use of intravenous injections of methedrine. [*Who instructed Bruce? No one in particular, it seems.*]

By contrast to the stance of Strunk and White and Orwell, the grammarian Otto Jespersen takes a downright expansive view of the passive voice and manages to come up with five situations that justify one's speaking in it. Often, for example, the doer of the deed described in a sentence can't be identified, and recourse to the passive eliminates the syntactical need to *say* who it was. In the passive, we can make do with "He was killed in the Boer War."

Even the broad-minded Jespersen, however, does not see—or, perhaps, sees but does not cite—psychotherapeutic grounds for use of the passive voice. Please bear with me as I blaze a path into that realm.

Consider these two sentences:

active voice
I won the Oscar for Best Actress.

passive voice
I was awarded the Oscar for Best Actress.

Think of all the factors besides talent that influence the members of the Academy of Motion Picture Arts and Sciences when they cast ballots for the year's best actress. A partial list:

- the actor pool they have to select from (Most films produced in a given year get little exposure, even to members of the Academy, and actors in those films are therefore effectively out of the running at Oscar time.)
- likeability or friendship
- envy
- sympathy (especially for older actors who've been bypassed for awards)
- box office receipts.

Which of the two formulations, active or passive, reflects more understanding of the whole context in which awards are made? The phrase "I won" seems to reduce a vast, complicated array of factors to just one factor (albeit a big one): talent—or perhaps talent coupled with will and hard work. It seems to say, "This was essentially my doing." Does the woman who says "I won"—even if her success indeed rests largely on her own talent—grasp her true bearings in relation to the world?

She does not, I think. The woman with true bearings is the second of the two, who, consciously or unconsciously, allows for the support and interplay of all the other elements that contributed to her success and says, "I was awarded."

But there is even more to say for passivity. In fact, I'm just finally coming to the heart of this chapter: Not only does it take a somewhat passive mindset to see the many things at work on one's behalf in life *besides* one's inborn gifts, but *those inborn gifts themselves can't be tapped without one's learning to be largely passive in relation to them.*

Artists, in particular, have led the way in giving expression to this insight, although it applies to all pursuits I know of.

At a post-performance Q and A session, I once heard puppeteer Eric Bass compellingly describe how, when performing, he "took his lead from" his puppet. And, in fact, his consummate performance *had* left me wondering who was in charge onstage, Bass himself or his loquacious wooden handful. "Art well concealed," you may say, but there was more—a profoundly deferential state of mind, an attitude embedded in the phrase "took my lead from."

Artists of all kinds are hesitant to say that they "produce" their creations. When they don't call on the passive voice to describe their work—as in such commonplaces as "I was inspired to . . . " or "gripped by . . . " or "flooded with . . . "— they resort to other ways to minimize their part in the process: phraseology like "I took my lead from" and "I felt I was channeling a source I couldn't name."

Sculptors who carve marble might be thought to be unlikely advocates of passivity in art. Isn't hacking into any solid piece of stone—to transform its shape forever—blatantly a case of imposing one's will on it? As a class, however, sculptors of marble aren't an exception to the rule.

Michelangelo, in fact, claimed that, in sculpting, he was merely *finding* forms concealed within his slabs. And Michelangelo's admirer Auguste Rodin talked of his own sculpture in the same, unmistakably passive spirit:

> The work of art is already in the marble. I
> just chop off the material that isn't needed.

What these artists have discovered is of crucial importance in all our endeavors, from beautifying women's hair . . . and selecting jurors for a trial who would view one's client sympathetically . . . to chicken-sexing (the job of sorting newborn chicks by sex, when the telling organs in question aren't yet displayed—a task at which the best practitioners can't say why they are succeeding).

Much of the time, even fighter pilots must rely on unconscious muscle memory, rather than on effortful (and time-consuming) calculation, when flying.

Does my reader still need assurance that the unconscious can play vital roles in life? Here, then, is more evidence to mull: We never learned consciously—learned, that is, by articulated rules—how to recognize a face or to throw both arms in front of ourselves to break a fall. These skills came to us with being human.

Or, try deciphering this passage:

. . . I cdnuolt blveiee taht I cluod aulaclty uesdnatnrd waht I was rdanieg. Aoccdrnig to a rscheeachr at Cmabrigde Uinervtisy, it deosn't mttaer in waht oredr the ltteers in a wrod are, the olny iprmoatnt tihng is taht the frist and lsat ltteer be in the rghit pclae.

I am guessing you succeeded, but how did you do it? You don't know. In all likelihood, little intellectual exertion was involved. The correct words came to you by a mechanism beyond consciousness—that same one briefly alluded to in the last sentence of the oddly spelled block quote itself.

And consider what goes into stringing adjectives together like this:

> eighty self-important state representatives

or like this:

> their big, well-written 2020 travel guide.

You could not have said,

> eighty state self-important representatives

or

> their well-written big travel 2020 guide

or, worse yet,

> big travel 2020 well-written their guide.

Linguists and grammarians have teased out the extremely complicated rules for sequencing adjectives in a series, but you and I and those grammarians themselves mastered those rules without ever being taught them or having them formulated for us. We absorbed them from all the conversations that we heard around us, and the process bypassed consciousness completely. Now, as we talk or poke away at keyboards, they have their way through us.

One reason many of us don't build much passivity into our activity is that we don't give the dark unconscious—what Michael Polanyi calls "the tacit dimension"—its full due. In compulsively standing guard against unreason (of course, to some extent we have to be on guard in that direction, since consequential bad decisions periodically descend on us from those same creviced hills in the brain), we deny ourselves access to the region where—alongside unappreciated mundane skills like sequencing adjectives and breaking a fall—many of our best, most valuable resources for creative life reside: instincts and dim memories, unpredictable associations . . . . Too forcible a feeling of "being in charge" somehow drives these into hiding.

In my own case, this discovery occurred in conditions I'd never have predicted for it: I was on a plane flight of about six hours, from Boston to L.A., at an altitude of more than thirty thousand feet. Until that flight, I had little inkling of what my unconscious abilities were. The echoing words of my elementary school principal, "Larry makes up in effort what he lacks in intelligence," had actually helped convince me at age ten never to trust my spontaneous instincts. I would compensate for meager brains by doing what I knew already how to do quite well: making plans and sticking to them. This itself was a comprehensive plan for life—a plan to go on planning—and its grip on me persisted far too long. I lived too single-mindedly, deliberately, with little "give," well into my twenties. Then came those six hours on a jet. I had been trying my hand as a playwright at the time but producing hardly any material that felt stageworthy to me. Then, to my astonishment, in my half-a-dozen airborne hours I turned out more text worth keeping than I had in all the several prior months of work on my project. What conditions had produced such a breakthrough? Once in California, I took walks along the ocean to process my experience. I came to believe two things:

- Being on a moving plane had, strangely enough, relieved me of my constant, proactive wish to be "getting somewhere." That, by definition, is what I was doing on a plane in motion. I could then relax and, relinquishing control of things in general, take a flight-within-a-flight, as well, aboard my unconscious.
- Means might well exist at ground level, too, for eliciting the state of mind that I enjoyed in flight.

That's when I began to make a point of saying, in my new, passive voice, "I *am being visited* by some ideas today, at my desk here," and "I've become *absorbed* by what a tragic fix my characters are getting into this morning," and the like.

In my own case—maybe yours, as well, so give it a try— what it mostly takes to tap into the stream of subliminal content is to replace active voice utterance with passive voice at certain moments. For me, that straightforward grammatical move brings generativity.

Also, for good measure, I keep a homemade sign on my desk that (only half-jokingly) reads, "You are being *paid* to be passive. Get used to it."

Active-Passive Hybrid No. I

Blessing

I hope not to be misunderstood here. My effort in the preceding chapter to resuscitate regard for the *passive* voice isn't meant to take away from the case I made earlier for use of the *active* voice. To my understanding, passivity needs somehow to be *mixed* with proactivity, if we are to live ably and happily.

In his poem "Ash Wednesday," T. S. Eliot writes, "Teach us to care and not to care," and those words express our deep aspiration to reconcile the responsible (that is, diligent, morally "in charge") life of agency with a life of receptivity. Complete passivity is, quite literally, death, but nonstop agency results in shoddy outcomes and a form of hell within. Until we learn to have it both ways, we fall short of human-kind's innate potential.

It may be true that

David Ortiz hit the baseball.

It is equally true that

> The sight of a baseball hurtling toward him at
> 95 mph in a vector sure to pass right through
> his strike zone triggered the great slugger's
> passive, unself-conscious reflex to swing.

It is for this reason linguist Benjamin Lee Whorf refers to popular belief in self-reliance as resting on the "naïve notion of an actor who produces an action." As Whorf knew, it's not as simple as that.

Unfortunately, though, English is sorely lacking in grammatical constructions that do justice to the active-passive hybrid state of mind involved in pulling off most real deeds on Earth. Sentence after sentence, our language *forces us to choose* between active voice and passive voice. Most of us pay dearly for this forced choice.

A curious—and beautiful—exception is the formula that always begins with the auxiliary subjunctive verb *may*:

> May your spirits lift.

> May the training center we break ground
> for on this day enable hundreds of young
> people to acquire skills that launch them on
> careers which enrich both themselves and
> this community.

What can be said to be happening by way of this locution?

In each case, the speaker expresses a wish. But in saying "May your spirits lift," rather than "I hope your spirits lift," he or she seems almost to be exercising jurisdiction in the matter. The phrase *I hope* does only what it says; it expresses hope. But *may* goes beyond mere desire; it lends the whole utterance a sense of fiat or bestowal.

Insofar as I can tell, the blessing formula using *may* does several things at once:

- it associates the speaker with a certain wish or vision, which she names;
- it implicitly acknowledges that she, all by herself, doesn't have sufficient power to bring the wished-for outcome to pass; and
- it invites the forces, people, or divinities whose help is required for that outcome to come into play.

If this understanding is correct, then blessings operate like Sanskrit mantras: They invoke. For example, by intoning "Kreeeeeeeeeeeeeemmmmmmmm," which is the sound associated with the Hindu goddess Kali, one calls upon—and welcomes—that fearsome deity to invade one's spirit or soul and destroy the negative forms of ego to be found there. The welcome itself is active; the openness to what that welcome brings is passive. Perhaps the reason David Ortiz was so good at what he did professionally for so long is that internally he always waited in a place of *may* as the ball approached him.

Are there grammatical formulas for blending active and passive in English I'm not thinking of—other ones a young, would-be David Ortiz could use to activate his whole, active/ passive self at home plate? We stand in need of them, not just to enhance our performance in a sport but to improve it in all activities we value, from plumbing to parenting.

For now, the wisest course available to us might be to keep our daily discourse well changed up, frequently mixing active and passive constructions, so that we both (a) report more truly on the complexity and causal uncertainty of the stories we tell and (b) get ourselves in better trim to go either way—passive or active—to address imbalance at a moment's notice. (Consider, for example, the toggling from passive to active in these sentences: "Ortiz *was transfixed* by the sight of the ball hurtling toward him at 95 mph. At a certain split second, *it triggered* his response to swing, *and he swung. He hit* the decisive home run that day.")

In the next chapter, I describe a distinctive form of active/passive alternation.

Active-Passive Hybrid No. 2

Emily Dickinson's Dashes

Emily Dickinson unsettles her readers with her punctuation. At hundreds of points that you and I would have thought called for commas, periods, or nothing at all, Dickinson puts dashes.

> Pain—has an Element of Blank—
> It cannot recollect
> When it begun—or if there were
> A time when it was not—

About Dickinson's mechanics, her first editor, Thomas Wentworth Higginson, wrote, "When a thought takes one's breath away, a lesson on grammar seems an impertinence." But her dashes, those intrusive horizontal lines of ink, so annoyed Higginson and other early editors of the poems that they took it upon themselves to delete and replace many of them. The original printing of the above stanza, edited by Higginson and Mabel Loomis Todd, changes all the punctuation, as well as two words. It reads,

> Pain has an Element of Blank;
> It cannot recollect
> When it began, or if there were
> A day when it was not.

Scholars have advanced theories to explain—or explain away—Dickinson's dashes. One such theory features their rhythmic value, another their being a means to juxtapose ostensibly unrelated elements in Dickinson's poems. But neither explanation bears close scrutiny, it seems to me.

A more plausible conjecture—one that leads me back to the passivity one needs for creativity—is that of R. W. Franklin, who dismisses the poet's use of them as a mere "habit of handwriting," pointing out the many that appear on an archived recipe of hers.

There *is* such a habit of the hand. It corresponds to the vocalization "Ummm," which, although speech coaches try to drum it out of their clients as a distracting interrupter, has the virtue of enabling a speaker to remain in passive (or "receiving") mode longer than she would otherwise. "My recipe for trout almondine," says a vital, active/passive Dickinson-like spirit, "uses butter, thin-sliced almonds, lemon juice, and—." One can *hear* this dash. It goes, "Ummm." It says, in effect, "The next ingredient I need will come to mind if I but let it . . . with my motor idling."

As in recipes, so, too, with poems, in Dickinson's case. I conceive her writing her first stanza on the subject "pain" in the midst of an excruciating toothache or migraine, each dash representing her attempt to catch a bit more meaning in the throbbing that assails her.

She begins,

Pain—

That first dash, I now take to signify, "Pain, I'm on call to you. Tell me what there is in you for me to hear, as I bide my time at this small table." Such a quiet and yet willful invocation is the active half of the creative hybrid—think of it as "tuning in."

The passive half, then, is the letting go and *being* "all ears" for the duration—thereby making good on what, implicitly, one promises to do by tuning in.

On those days when the poet's (or the architect's or doctor's) stars are in alignment, that alchemical one-two maneuver yields a slew of unanticipated, fine results. "Yes," the poet gratefully whispers, entering her zone as she writes, "Pain . . . has an Element of Blank—."

And then, "That's right," she says, with her second dash. "What else of your essential nature, Pain, might I get you to confide in me if, by showing how invested in this sheet of paper I've become—through applying still more ink to it *between* words—I express my faith in you to *have* more for me?"

Every one of Dickinson's quarter-inch-long horizontal marks is, if I am right, a gesture full of will and agency that, paradoxically enough, aims at nothing but resumption of passivity, a finely tuned receptivity to truths new to her. Think of it as her left arm, extended horizontally to hold a front porch door ajar for company she's never met.

Wasn't it Dickinson who, elsewhere, told us, "Not knowing when the dawn will come, I open every door"?

GRAMMAR FOR
BELONGING

I f, on occasion, I feel at peace with the universe, that probably has less to do with my fitness for a strange, vast, and volatile cosmos than it does with the reception I happen to be getting at the time from beings of my own kind.

As Sigmund Freud and others point out, in one's infancy, one's mother is a person's whole world. Then, however, society takes over, playing the sustaining parent to us after we've been weaned.

What Mom provided us at first is, in adulthood, proffered on all sides by surrogates: For protection, we now have the police; for milk, the dairy section of a market; and for affection, a mate. Without belonging to a family or close friendship group, workplace, and town, the individual would be hard put to meet his psychic and material needs in life.

As I quoted earlier, Hillel once rhetorically asked, "If I am not for myself, who will be?" He didn't leave the matter there, however, but went on to ask, "If I'm for myself alone, what am I?" Even just to have "a name on file"—a well-fixed identity on Earth—necessitates there being others in my life and some give-and-take between us.

That is, we human beings have abundant good reason for use of the first-person plural, we. It transforms us lone creatures into members of *a collective whose benefits are mutual—that is, a community. The use of we is the invaluable linguistic move being made when a five-year-old boy—having successfully offered himself as a replacement for an absent peer, the usual fourth player in a game of foursquare at recess—proves himself adequate, then says, "We can play this way tomorrow, too, okay?" With his we, the boy boldly puts his isolation behind him.*

That same move is underway when a woman who's upset about crop-duster planes spraying harmful chemicals in her area gets on the phone to neighbors whom she barely knows and says (by and by), "I feel just like you do on this issue. We should organize."

We, then, reflects the need for belonging— not just belonging in a group, but belonging in the cosmos through a group. And it reflects the need of the individual to band with others when she can't possibly achieve a certain aim singlehandedly.

Wondrous Touch

Elements of Audibility

I never had a reason to doubt that my mother adored me until she started writing letters to me at college.

Mistakenly believing that quotation marks can be used for emphasis, she would close each letter with the line, "You know how much we 'love' you."

She thought she was making me feel loved, but the whole thing put me in mind of the B. B. King song "Nobody Loves Me but My Mother, and She Could Be Jivin', Too."

At the same time, although Mom was somewhat off in her *selection* of a piece of grammar that would touch me, she wasn't wrong at all in her belief that "touching" one's reader is a demonstrable feat in grammar's bag of tricks.

The fact that grammar has that capability is an important boon to us, in light of our enduring need for tactile company. That need is prehistoric in its origins—physiological, in fact. If, as infants, we don't get an ample dose of what transactional psychologists call stroking—if, that is, we're deprived of nurturing contact with members of our own species (picture chimps diligently grooming each other)—we are unlikely to thrive in life. That's how we've been wired, say the neurobiologists.

As we leave our infancy and head on up the road toward adulthood, we begin acquiring means to satisfy the need for stroking besides literal, physical contact. In particular, *words* stroke us—almost any words, even commonplaces uttered by strangers at a Dunkin' Donuts or Starbucks, like "Excuse me, but is that used newspaper yours?"—if they're addressed to us in person. Such words represent our human world attending to us; we feel slightly caressed by them.

Amazingly—and here comes grammar's part—often we feel stroked even by the *written* words of people. We feel stroked by the intimate effect created on a page when its absent author works traces of her own *voice* into the language—say, the dismissive finality of certain grammatical fragments, like "No way!" and "Over my dead body!" or the confidential tone of a parenthesis, like that in "He's a Pisces (need I say more?)." John Trimble, author of *Writing with Style*, calls this voice effect "warm, imaginative touch."

That's what my mother had been wanting to transmit to me with her misguided quote marks.

Nor is such fictitious body heat felt only by one's readers. Having done my share of "voicing" on paper and online over the years, I can attest to its salutary effect on me myself, the writer, too. By use of voice, I, in a sense, reenter the space that my readers and I have shared physically—or that I imagine we share—anticipating their stopped breath or nods or appreciative laughter. I feel that I am doing more than imparting my ideas: I am paying an enjoyable visit. I'm keeping up the sociable side of myself.

It takes practice to vocalize in writing. As the late Prof. Walker Gibson, who wrote extensively about tone and persona, explained,

> Someone walks in the door and we throw a greeting at him—or her. We can say HELLo, meaning I'm a bored and irascible fellow, or I'm kiddingly pretending to be, and O golly, you again! We can say hello, cheerfully, meaning you and I are friendly enough but not really intimate. Or we can say hellooo, which defines, of course, quite a different speaker and quite a different relation.

In speech, these "hellos" are made distinct from one another through specific uses of the voice box and face, which linguists have dubbed *kinesics*. "The trouble with the written word," says Gibson, "is that it comes to us without kinesics—no voice box, no eyebrows." According to him, "The writer's task is to so surround his words with other words on the page that his reader may infer the quality of the desired speaking voice."

Making up in writing for writing's inaudibility is largely a matter of word choice—replacing "I would be delighted to" with "Sure, anytime," or (moving in the opposite direction, toward *more* formality) replacing "party" with "upcoming social event." However, punctuation and syntax play their parts, as well. In fact, the modern system of punctuation introduced by the Italian printer Aldus Manutius (1450–1515) was largely an attempt to invest writing with speech effects like pauses and relative emphasis.

Without knowing it, an anonymous fan of the TV soap opera *Guiding Light* proved herself a more-than-worthy heir of Manutius and his fellow printer/innovators when, in 1982, she wrote to the show's producers. She put quotation marks around a word to make herself sound bemused, employed an exclamation mark to make herself sound surprised, worked in a two-word interrupter set off by commas ("you know") for a scolding touch, and even willfully misspelled a word (the word "please") to ensure that it got heard as she would have said it.

Gentlemen:

Here I am actually "hooked" on a program, to the extent of not even accepting an invitation if it means not being able to see my program! . . .

The little lady that plays Nola Reardon is a darling, beautiful child—and certainly should go places. While she plays a difficult part, she actually makes you live the story with her.

Puhlease—don't let her do any more damage. Tell your writers to let her mend her ways.

If you care about fostering a sense of community between us—a sense of shared presence—don't just *write* to me. In your writing, *be* that person who you are in the flesh.

Clear Messaging

Marks and Modifiers that Go Missing . . . and Much More

One shouldn't aim at being possible to understand, but at being impossible to misunderstand.

— QUINTILIAN

I can almost hear my former colleagues laughing at my having gotten this far into a book about grammar without dealing with grammar's basic function—making ourselves clear to each other. Please take my word for it that I had no intention to neglect communication entirely, since it definitely has as much to do with personal well-being as the less familiar uses of grammar do.

When we get too lax grammatically, words take on meaning unintended by their speakers. If they are the words a friend has used in giving us directions, we lose our way en route to a parade. If they are the words in a manufacturer's set of assembly instructions, we end up sitting on a wobbly chair for years.

Worse than that, on account of certain instances of disregard for grammar, we find ourselves in needless arguments with one another.

Every such failure in the transmission of meaning makes society feel a bit less useful to us and less caring. We feel "unheard," as we say.

A typical "bad grammar day" might begin with a *misplaced modifier*. A man—I'll call him Bud—mulls what to wear on an unusually cold autumn morning. No sooner does he tentatively don an old jacket of his than his wife pipes up, "Being in such poor shape, you really shouldn't wear that." She means the jacket is in poor shape, but her word order leaves Bud thinking that it's him—or his belly in particular—that she has in mind. His workouts at the gym, he thinks, have probably not had the good effect on his physique that he'd imagined.

Unhappily commuting to work that morning, Bud then sees a new sign on the highway, one obviously timed for the arrival of winter in a few weeks: "Plows Use Caution." Since it has no internal punctuation, his first reading of it—which he rapidly dismisses as implausible—is that, for some reason, the Department of Public Works is congratulating its own snowplowing crews on their past record of safety.

He decides that there must be an internal comma or period missing after *Plows*, but he can't be sure which of those two marks it is. If a comma—and the sign was meant to read, "Plows, Use Caution"—*Plows* is a noun of address, and the sign is practically the opposite of kudos: It's a reminder to the DPW's operators of snow plows to *take* care on the road, so as not to damage cars into whose lanes their large blades often protrude. If, though, it's a period that's missing after *Plows*—and the sign was meant to read, "Plows. Use Caution"—it's the drivers of mere normal vehicles, like Bud himself, who are being addressed: "Plows" is a sentence fragment meaning "You'll see plows out on this road again this winter," and "Use Caution" is a warning to Bud and other motorists to give those plows a wide berth.

In a word, Bud finds the orthographic issues raised so distracting that he misses his turnoff.

When at last Bud shows up at his job, our linguistic everyman is treated to a bit of prose with *another* type of punctuation missing. That prose specimen is a rare email to Bud from his company's president:

> Bud, I ran into Sven Johnson at the game last night. He said, "Bud's project team is reaching all the wrong conclusions. I disagree.

Bud would pay good money to know exactly where in this message Sven Johnson's words end, but Bud's inattentive boss has not inserted an end-quotation mark after Sven's words. If the sentence "I disagree" is Sven's, it is Sven's way of underscoring how wrong Bud's conclusions are, and the boss, in letting Sven's words speak for themselves, is probably expressing concern about Bud's work. If, on the other hand, the sentence "I disagree" is the boss's own, it's his means of parting company with Sven and giving Bud a vote of confidence!

Soon enough, however, Bud himself is making contributions to the world's syntactical confusion. To his assistant he sends a text containing a *pronoun reference problem*:

> When Jane Fonda-Bonardi comes to you today with her guest, Mrs. Singh from India, please tell Jane that I would like to see her.

By "her," he means Jane, but his assistant takes "her" to be the Indian guest. The mistake will cost Bud twenty awkward minutes with said Mrs. Singh later in the day.

Then, upon too blithely hitting his send button, our good Bud is out the door. Walking in the sharp, brisk air between buildings, he espies a colleague who's impatient for some help from him on a special project—Bud has had to put it off until January, by which time he hopes to have completed other work accumulating on his desk. As he and that colleague pass, Bud—wanting just to show that he has not forgotten his promise—delivers a *fragment out of context* to his skeptical co-worker. He (reassuringly, he thinks) points an index finger upward and says, "January!" She, though, strangely responds, "Oh yes, terrible."

Presently, but not in time, it registers with Bud that she has taken his curt, one-word sentence "January!" as a comment on the weather they're both walking through, which is too cold for November.

It isn't 10:00 a.m. yet, and the wheels of verbal havoc are at full spin. By 5:00 p.m., a veritable fog of words and marks—light in some locales, thick in others—has descended on the land, and the few common errors cited above account for but a small fraction of it.

Other grammatical pitfalls range from *double negatives* and *tense shifts* to egregious *run-on sentences*. Nongrammatical mistakes include the use of terms that simply will not mean what their speakers want them to.

Can it be a mere coincidence that so much of the word *message* consists of *mess*?

The effect of our grammatical mismanagement is sometimes humorous. (The headline writer who entitled an obituary "Chester Morrill Was Fed Secretary" would have us believe that the late top official at the Federal Reserve Bank will be remembered mainly for an unwitting act of cannibalism.) Other times, lack of care with grammar does real harm.

Consider, for instance, the man who, in writing his will, stipulates that proceeds from the eventual sale of his home be "divided evenly between my son Carlos and my twins." What was his intent? By grouping two of his three children together as "my twins," did he mean to have them treated as a unit for purposes of probate, so that Carlos alone and *the twins together as a unit* would each receive a half of the estate? That reading would oblige the twins to split their share.

Anyone who's known of petty, fraught relationships within a family will have little trouble imagining the years-long strife that can result from such uncertainty.

In wills, in the operating manuals that come with new appliances, and in treaties made between antagonistic nations, even a misplaced comma sometimes causes damage out of all proportion to its throw-weight in ink.

On that cautionary note, I end my appeal for care in avoiding grammar's traps and snares. There is no denying the importance of clear, unobstructed transmission of ideas, even from the standpoint of our mental health and thriving. (Just imagine what a different day my "Bud" might have had if his wife had said, "Being in such poor shape, *that jacket* needs replacing"—and if his boss had written, "Sven said, 'Bud's project team is reaching all the wrong conclusions.' I disagree.")

Still, I hesitate to give the grammatical obstacles to clarity more space here for two reasons: First, the interested reader can find countless good, whole books devoted *just* to those snags, such as certain books by Richard Lederer and Lynne Truss. Second, my chief reason for producing *this* book was to take up properties of grammar more surprising.

Bonding

Ellipses

I think of the late, sweet folk-blues singer Mississippi John Hurt as the man who made the dots of the ellipsis (...) into notes of music.

The first and maybe second time he came to a song's refrain, he'd sing all the words. In later repetitions, though, it could be hard to predict which of those words would escape his lips and which would be left to the listener's short-term memory as Mississippi John fell silent, letting his guitar sing for him. He might leave out the refrain's first words or its last. Nor was he above going suddenly mute in its middle, then vocally "coming back on" as he was moved to.

It always seemed appropriate that his ellipses be rendered as pleasing instrumental sounds. At its best, the ellipsis is, among other things, a form of celebration, an inspired way of deepening community. *The ellipsis shows us that, to some degree at least, communal bonds exist already, since certain facts pertaining to the speaker and/or listener "go without saying" between them.*

In verbal terms, intimacy starts and grows there.

One point to keep in mind is that ellipses aren't always signaled by those dots I mentioned (. . .), even in writing. In fact, usually they're not. Usually, the speaker just omits a bit of language and does nothing whatsoever to indicate his surreptitious deed.

Consider common pleasantries, for instance. "I'll see you later at Joe's house" gets contracted—as the speaker and her listener grow better acquainted—to "See you at Joe's." And with still more familiarity, all that may be left of the original, seven-word sentence is one lone word: "Later."

Having greater bonding power, though, are the elliptical "pointers": words and phrases like *even*, *of all things*, and *ironically*. If I say in an email message, "Even my sister wanted to sign the get-well card to Mrs. O'Hara," I am using *even* as a way to let my correspondent know that I suspect he knows my family well enough to see at once what makes my sister's act remarkable; there's no need to tell him. If I say "My sister, of all people, refused to have wine," I am doing much the same; I am practically declaring my friend to be a close extension of my kin.

It is, to a large extent, the ellipsis which accounts for the joyful, bonding power inherent in the telling of a good joke.

In a magazine, I once saw an impressionistic painting of a port in France. I so liked it that I tore it out to frame it. Only, it was laid out horizontally, and for the wall I had in mind for it I needed something vertical, so I cropped it liberally at both side ends, never considering that certain artist types among my acquaintances might notice. When they do, I put on the most defensive, hurt tone that I can, saying, "Hey, no, look, it's a Monet. I couldn't afford the whole thing, all right?"

If, as I hope, a person laughs at this, her laughter's source is subterranean. It's in what she understands without my having said it—about my financial means to buy even a square inch of a Monet, about the absurdity of cutting such a painting into pieces in the first place, etc. It's also in her tacit knowledge that, in fact, I'm play-acting: She knows both that I am lying and that I assume she *knows* I'm lying.

Last but hardly least, *love* comes into view here, as a beneficiary of the ellipsis.

In our most intimate relationships, of course, a great deal goes without saying.

For example, I am now convinced that one of the most widely anthologized elliptical poems in English is, aptly enough, a love poem. It's by William Carlos Williams:

> This Is Just to Say
>
> I have eaten
> the plums
> that were in
> the icebox
> and which
> you were probably
> saving
> for breakfast
> Forgive me
> they were delicious
> so sweet
> and so cold

Incredibly, in the margin of the book where a young and callow me first found this poem, all I say about it is "plums." I had not been married yet.

Put yourself in the place of Williams's wife, Flossie. How blatantly outrageous on this greedy husband's part to add insult to injury by telling her the plums he had deprived her of were a great treat, in his opinion—unless, that is, his real intent was to celebrate their love for one another.

Between Williams's mischievous lines, I hear him saying, "I feel so certain of our staying power as a couple that I have no fear even of reminding you of what a problematic choice of spouse you made."

But that was in the kitchen. Does elliptical language crop up in such rooms as the bedroom, as well?

And how, it does.

Foreplay in particular is not often the ideal occasion for complete sentences, even between life partners who, in their daytime personae, are sticklers with grammar. As e. e. cummings writes,

> [The person] who pays any attention
> to the syntax of things
> will never wholly kiss you.

Let's take our lead from the loving likes of William Carlos Williams and e. e. cummings. We can make rhythmically calculated use of silence to mark, revel in, and build upon the good things that are gaining hold between us.

A Defense of Correctness

Apostrophes

Mind your p's and q's.

— A LEGENDARY, OFT-QUOTED
SCHOOLMARM

Not all grammatical errors in this world sow confusion.

If I write,

> Those first, trend-setting computer enthusiast's obsession was games like Pac-Man.

I violate the rule to place an apostrophe *after* the final "s" of a possessive noun, rather than before it, when that possessive is plural. If I start a sentence,

> Sallys obsession wasn't the primitive business apps—

Empathizing

The Apostrophe Errors Made by Other People

I t's one thing to hold *oneself* to standards of correctness, quite another to hold one's fellow human beings to account, as grammar sticklers do.

I have been a teacher by profession, but a much-neglected fact of social life is that every one of us is part teacher. One reason we live in groups at all is to benefit from others' correction of us as we get our bearings on Earth and grow into competent adults. It's only through ongoing feedback of our parents, schoolteachers, and advice-dispensing friends that we are capable of sewing, hunting, or balancing a checkbook, let alone designing houses for ourselves.

Even so, correction that we do unmindfully, without empathy, can produce more harm than good; it can actually induce people we care about to give up on pursuits in which, with time, they could have performed at high levels.

The seven-year-old girl on a soccer team who has spent the last year eager to be old enough to play, quits after two weeks during which her mother and/or coach has loudly castigated her from the sidelines for forgetting not to use her hands. A novice attorney (yes, lawyers whom I've known have feelings, too) sees his deep attraction to the law go up in smoke on studying the latest unrelenting, long critique of one of his first briefs by a senior partner. Kinder guidance might have shepherded his promising career on to its fruition.

Grammar is a realm made to order for developing the teaching skills we *all* require, off and on, when helping less experienced co-workers, friends, and family members. I say this because every person who, like me, has mastered some few dozen rules of grammar stands in constant danger of becoming a negative force in the life of the uninitiated. Just as with the rabid soccer mom and impatient senior partner in my examples, many of us trigger-happy wielders of red pens must curb our ways or stop pretending to be playing one of our community's most sacred roles, that of mentor.

This was brought home to me early in my teaching career, and in words I'm unlikely ever to forget. I had spent my whole first conference with a recent refugee from Vietnam diligently circling—and freely expounding on—every possessive in her paper crying out for an apostrophe, every modifier she'd misplaced, every word she hadn't used idiomatically . . . . At the end of it, the student, who had noticed that few of my comments were positive and that none had to do with her paper's substance, stood up from her chair avoiding my gaze. As she put her paper away, she said (in a valiant, broken English), "Do you know? You have treat me like dummy."

As her boldness with me will attest, this young woman was at least somewhat fortified against my type. What of all the students in my colleagues' and my classes—and the employees of a callous boss, children of overworked parents, and so on—who've endured similar demeaning treatment at another's hands but internalized it? One reeling and demoralized student at my college told his counselor that he felt he was a "C-minus on two legs."

In order to continue to develop—in order, that is, to make good *use* of correction—a person needs to be assured (or to know already, from long experience) that his corrector holds both him and his not-yet-displayed, latent abilities in high regard.

If you're my age, you recall the bumper sticker that denounced nuclear energy: "Split Wood, Not Atoms." I'd like to see one reading, "Split Infinitives—Not the Human Beings

Who Produce Them." But there would have to be small print on such a sticker explaining *how* picayune correction splits a human being. It would read, "Nobody should be cut off from the inner well of confidence required to get on in this world."

Or perhaps a better catchphrase for bumpers would be "Grammar, What Big Teeth You Have."

How might someone go about correcting others, in light of all I've just said? Some alternatives occur to me. Although my context for presenting them will be the process of mastering grammar, I trust that my reader will see how these approaches can be brought to bear in fostering mastery of every skill that matters.

One option is the way recommended by a Roman emperor, of all people. In his *Meditations*, Marcus Aurelius gratefully names some twenty individuals who have provided him with models for how to live. There, amid the most august personages of the time, the reader also finds a man whose chief legacy to Aurelius was the example he set for how to respond to a grammatical error without disrespecting the person who commits it.

> 10. From Alexander the grammarian, [I learned] to refrain from fault-finding, and from chiding those who utter any [wrong] expression. [I learned how, instead,] to dexterously model the very expression that ought to have been used by the speaker—and by way of answering him, giving confirmation to him, or

decide not to let the last five words here be a sentence of their own?"—it became clear that this student *knew* he shouldn't join two complete thoughts in the same sentence that way. This too-diligent member of my class had let his clauses "run on" simply because he did not *consider* "they choke in the end" a complete thought. If it stood alone, he asked me, how could any reader tell who "they" was? Which is to say, this young man was taking the standard of "completeness" far more literally than you or I or 99.9% of English speakers would ever dream of doing.

In a word, I have gone from seeing grammatical repeat offenders as folks who are *careless* of our verbal laws to seeing most of them as overzealous *enforcers* of the law . . . as they understand it.

I like them better that way: They remind me more of me—or at least of me in my obsessive moments. When they're wrong, they're likely to have erred by being too nervously cautious or logical. I need to treat them with a due regard for their conscientiousness. I need to say, "It interests me that you insert a question mark after your sentence 'I now wonder about fairness in the U.S. tax code.' Can you tell me why?" (That word "wonder" is probably a clue, but maybe not.) Or, "You write, 'There was not no hatred in that woman.' Why do you say 'not no,' rather than just 'not' or just 'no'?" (The answer might well be that "not no" is more emphatic—a justification for the double negative in many dialects and languages—or it may have absolutely nothing to do with that.)

The need for empathy in a community is often best served by assuming that Socrates's dictum still holds: If a person *knew* what's right to do, he or she would now be doing it.

Generosity

Semicolons, Cumulative Sentences

Sometime last year, I found myself on the campus of a great university whose main administrative building was being renovated.

Needing certain tickets that were available only at the information center normally housed in that now-barricaded building, I managed to find a security guard at the site and asked him where the office I needed was now located. He (unwittingly, I think) launched me on a far-flung wild goose chase in surrounding streets, which ended with my finally discovering the information center in its temporary quarters at the rear of the same building I had started at.

As a student working there went looking for the tickets I needed, I made bold to broach the situation with one of her peers behind the counter, quietly saying, "By the way, did I miss a sign on the front of the building directing me here?"

"No," he said, "there's no sign there." At which point, I paused politely to allow either him or a nearby co-worker who'd been eavesdropping to follow up with words like "We should really do something about that." No such comment was forthcoming.

In the kindest voice I have, I then ventured, "It's a shame, though, isn't it, to be sending people in circles?" And I paused again before saying, "Especially an information center. You might think an office of this nature would—I mean, conceivably—take a special interest in providing needed information."

In short, no one on the premises seemed to catch what I was getting at, or care. These young people were, I told myself, in danger of swelling the already well-populated ranks of adults who "work to rule," doing little more than what the law and their respective job descriptions require of them. One might call them civic minimalists.

What can I say? When they remain like that, such fellow citizens live out their lives at one extreme of interpersonal myopia, but few of us possess the big heart we would like to have—the expansive, giving disposition that, from time to time in life, a relative or friend, even stranger, has displayed toward us, to address a need of ours they glimpsed. Whether on account of laziness, an inherited "shy gene," or traumatic times in childhood that taught us of the dangers that come with exposing ourselves, we may lack hearts of the right size for full participation in communal life.

Grammar offers two means to supplement a personal approach to heart enlargement. One is that notorious mark of punctuation so inscrutable to most people, the semicolon. The other is a sentence type too rarely employed in this age of sound bites: the cumulative sentence.

Though John Trimble sings the semicolon's praises in his *Writing with Style*, he worries out loud that the average first-year college student "isn't ready" for it. As an instructor of writing myself, I must agree that college students seem to misuse the mark more often than they use it correctly. They understand its function as super-divider in a series of items that also includes commas—as in "Tucson, Arizona; Fort Collins, Colorado; and Richmond, Virginia"—but its other, more discursive functions elude them.

The following excerpts of Albert Einstein and Annie Dillard all contain semicolons. I enter them into the record as instances of what that odd, earring-shaped mark connotes—at least to Dillard, Einstein, and me, if not to everyone: It signifies that one's largesse is not yet spent.

I present Einstein's semicolon first, which appears in his response to the generic layperson who has just been told what enormous energy is locked away in every unit of mass on Earth (namely, that mass multiplied by the speed of light squared, expressed in joules) and logically then wants to know how such potential force could possibly have gone unnoticed for so long. Einstein gives his unseen reader first a simple, apt analogy and then—with the insertion of that mark of punctuation which reveals a large, forthcoming spirit, the semicolon—goes on to make his point explicit, in case it has been missed.

> It is as though a man who is fabulously rich should never spend or give away a cent; no one could tell how rich he was.

the statement of the main clause or more often . . . explicate or exemplify it, so that the sentence has a flowing and ebbing movement, advancing to a new position and then pausing to consolidate it, leaping and lingering."

Compare the terse, cut-and-run, ungenerous effect of most sentences to the effect of the following cumulative line:

> If he ever runs again for office, Martinez will deal with his opponents' scurrilous attacks on him more forcefully, standing squarely in the middle of the fray, not malicious but unapologetic, always ready with fresh, unequivocal press releases that enlarge upon his refutation of the latest trumped-up charges and remind voters of his unique vision for the city's future.

Sentences like that are overflowing, open-ended systems.

Here's a better (and less partisan) specimen than mine, by an unnamed student of Francis Christensen:

> It was as though someone, somewhere, had touched a lever and shifted gears, and the hospital was set for night running, smooth and silent, its normal clatter and hum muffled, the only sounds heard in the white-walled room distant and unreal: a low hum of voices from the nurses' desk, quickly stifled, the soft squish of rubber-soled shoes on the tiled corridor, starched white cloth rustling

against itself, and, outside, the lonesome
whine of wind in the country night and the
Kansas dust beating against the windows.

By the time I finish writing such a sentence (when I
manage to), I can feel my chest swelling—not so much with
pride as with a new, giving disposition. "One day," I fancifully tell myself, "I'll be as big a soul as that great fount of
words and semicolons, Walt Whitman, whose generosity
expanded beyond the limits of words to take nonverbal form
as well." And I think of Whitman's unstinting service to
those suffering in Civil War infirmaries.

A REMINDER APPLYING TO THIS WHOLE BOOK

Will producing more cumulative sentences lead to "heart
enlargement" automatically? By no means.

Now may be the time to remind my reader that one's
spirit doesn't grow through practices enacted with no felt
sense of *intention* to affect spirit. Without appropriate
intention, a Catholic might as well ingest a wafer at mass
just to cancel out a sour taste left in her mouth from breakfast. Without "kavanah," a Jew may well be seen to *slap* his
skullcap to his head, in a thoughtless flurry on his way to
services that mark the weekly day of rest. As beautifully
conceived as any act may be in terms of its *potential* effect
on psychic well-being, that effect is not a likely outcome for
someone who doesn't yearn for it to some degree, or at least
extend it a true welcome.

To Compromise but Not Be "Compromised"

"They"—Made Singular

You can have my Oxford comma* when you pry it from my cold, dead, and lifeless hands.

— THE CRY OF DEFIANCE RECENTLY SEEN
PRINTED ON A MUG

. . . .

There is nothing stable in the world.

— JOHN KEATS

Correctness, it turns out, is a moving target.

Occasionally, one of the undergraduate writing tutors I supervised at Bentley University would put an arcane question of grammar to me, and I, if I happened to be at the top of my form that day, would answer him at

---

* This is the comma inserted after the second-to-last item in a series of three or more items, as in "cold, dead, and lifeless hands."

length. He and his fellows would then stare at me in that same, frozen state of awe reserved by deer for true luminaries. Once, terminating just such a pause, one tutor suddenly observed, "Larry, you are like a god."

In the flush of grammar glory, I sometimes forget to tell my acolytes that the so-called "rules" are nothing but reports of verbal usage out on the street these days, not the creation of scholars like myself.

I've yet to encounter the student adversary immortalized in John Barth's novel *The End of the Road*. He's a student of that book's protagonist, an intimidating professor of English. At the moment of their face-off, the professor is feeling "acute, tuned up, razor sharp." He has just managed to explain "the rules governing the case forms of English pronouns"—why, for example, one should say, "I was thought to be he," not "I was thought to be him." Then, from the back of his classroom, his nemesis chimes in, "Aw, look, which came first, the language or the grammar books?"

> "What's on your mind, Blakesley?" [the professor] demanded, refusing to play his game.
>
> "Well, it stands to reason people talked before they wrote grammar books, and all the books did was tell how people were talking. For instance, when my roommate makes a phone call I ask him, 'Who are you talking to?' Everybody in this class would say, 'Who are you talking to?' . . . Nobody's going to say, 'To whom were you just now

talking?' I'll bet even you wouldn't say it. It sounds queer, don't it?" The class snickered. "Now this is supposed to be a democracy, so if nobody but a few profs would ever say, 'To whom were you just now speaking?', why go on pretending we're all out of step but you? Why not change the rules?"

I can only hope that when my turn comes to deal with that challenge to authority, I display more candor than Barth's imaginary teacher goes on to summon. What the student here contends is mostly true: Usage leads the way; rules come along to reflect, validate, and stabilize usage temporarily. In other words, people follow rules, but only so long as they feel like it. Ultimately (unbeknownst to most of them), it's a nation's populace itself that has the upper hand.

Accordingly, in recent times, the ban against contractions such as "can't" and "she'll" in formal writing has been dropped. Also, just as Barth's fictional student claims, most educated writers have begun to speak of "someone who I know"—kissing *whom* good-bye. Will educated speakers one day also say, "That decision isn't fair to Josh and I," or "She and him went to the movies"? Quite possibly.

That's an unsettling prospect, all right. (Even just having to admit it to the waiting room of future possibilities results in a perceptible increase in my blood pressure.) In terms of personal growth, however, there's an upside to linguistic change: It can be the occasion for learning how to deal with change of all kinds in this world.

Of the changes now working their way through English, none is spreading faster than the use of the plural third-person pronoun *they* to do the work that logically belongs to a singular pronoun. The sentence

> A person who has undergone EMT training
> at Michigan knows what they're doing.

is likely to annoy a great many people who value precision in expression. How did the solitary thing *a person* morph into that multitude *they*?

Of course, we know the main reason for this change. In the singular, English is lacking for third-person pronouns covering both sexes. The traditional solution of defaulting to *he* when the gender is irrelevant or unknown—

> A person who has undergone EMT training
> at Michigan knows what he is doing.

—has fallen out of use as we've become aware that such practices attach more agency and competence to men than to women. The readiest-to-hand substitute for *he* (other than *she*, which simply reverses the bias) is *they*.

And now we're all starting to learn important lessons about gender fluidity and genderlessness. The call for alternatives only grows louder.

I'm all for alternatives—new ones, too—but I mightily resist the use of *they* as one, except when I'm referring to a friend who is non-binary. Although it has a long history, I pull out all manner of clumsier locutions to avoid seeming to confuse the single human being with the many. In my humble view, we have done too much homogenizing in our day already. (I spell this out at some length in my chapter "Having One's Own Way of Seeing," below.)

Professor of English Maxine Hairston—who lived much of her life on a ranch, where, I'm guessing, individuality was prized—identified six nonsexist alternatives to *he*, short of resorting to the blurring plural. In this book, I've employed all but one of her apt strategies.

- When feasible, use plural nouns and thereby eliminate the *need* to choose a pronoun of specific gender; often this is the simplest remedy. For example: "Painters who want to exhibit their work," not "A painter who wants to exhibit his work."
- Reword the sentence to eliminate the gendered pronoun. For example: "The average American drives a car three years," instead of "The average American drives his car three years."
- When feasible, substitute *one* for *he* or *she* or *man* or *woman*. For example: "If one plans ahead, one can retire at 60," instead of "If a man plans ahead, he can retire at 60."
- When it seems indicated, write *he or she* or *his or her*, as long as you don't use the phrases too often, they won't be conspicuous.
- If you wish, consistently write *he/she* and *him/her*.
- Sometimes use *she* and *her* instead of *he* and *him* as general pronouns. For example: "The driver who is

renewing her license must now pass an eye test," and "An officer who makes an arrest should show her badge."

Oh, I don't deny that in conversing with friends who say "they" in place of a singular pronoun, I will do the same at times. I might say,

> The accountant who pretends not to see blatant fraud in such a company's books only does so because they're afraid to lose that company as a paying client.

When I do, though, I always feel . . . well, not as compromised as the accountant in my example, but compromised to an extent. The accountant fears losing customers; I fear losing the friendship of folks I'm talking with. My self-regard would, I think, improve if I could somehow stop *feeling* compromised at those moments and start seeing them as opportunities for *learning* to compromise, within limits. After all, the need to compromise, within limits, is as much a fact of verbal life as it is a fact of social life generally. Like those famous arbiters of English usage, the Fowlers, in the end I "prefer geniality to grammar."

But I say "compromise, within limits" advisedly. I don't want to do mere mimicry, the unthinking *seizure* of locutions heard on others' lips. To me (please excuse the bit of moralizing that I feel coming on), thoughtless echoing is the verbal preparation for complicity in questionable acts of all sorts, ranging from a teenage group's ostracism of a peer it deems uncool to an engineer's signing off, under subtle pressure from her colleagues, on a product of their company known to be hazardous.

Where, then, can one look for guidance?

Maybe by tweaking some words of Eric Partridge on grammar, we can derive a principle that's not confined to grammar only. Grammar, says Partridge,

> must modify itself if language changes, grammar being made for man, not man for grammar.
>
> Nevertheless, where grammatical rules make for a clarity that would disappear with the disappearance of the rules, it is better to preserve and maintain the rules—until, at least, a more satisfactory rule [emerges].

Partridge's only criterion here is clarity. If, though, to clarity we added terms like mutual respect and joy, might we then not have the beginnings of a formulation that could be used for judging changes in our conduct generally, not just grammatical changes?

At any rate, that's what I am clinging to for steadiness right now.

GRAMMAR FOR FREEDOM

I have known the eyes already,
known them all—

The eyes that fix you in a
formulated phrase,

And when I am formulated,
sprawling on a pin,

When I am pinned and
wriggling on the wall,

Then how should I begin

To spit out all the butt-ends
of my days and ways?
— FROM "THE LOVE SONG
OF J. ALFRED PRUFROCK,"
BY T. S. ELIOT

The downside to being known by others is the likelihood of soon becoming a known quantity. T. S. Eliot's stanza on the spiritual cost of life in a community was the first snatch of modern poetry to surprise me with its resonance.

At the time, I was chafing at the ways I was being labeled by high school peers. As I grew older, those classmates were replaced by co-workers, bosses, students of my own, political constituents, and countless other specialists in sizing one up. To people who knew of my leadership in creating a school desegregation *plan, I was a champion of racial harmony. To hundreds who attended a meeting at which I opposed the appointment of a certain person of color to be the next principal of one of our city's schools, I was a racist.*

All too often, we take others' portrayals of ourselves—even others' gross distortions of us—and internalize them, add them to the stock of lines we use against ourselves inside our sound-proof minds, where, unheard, their effects cannot be checked by our best friends. In so doing, we become, to an extent, walking caricatures: the eternal Boy Scout, sycophant, martinet, house-wife, whore. (What is the psychology of this acceptance of demeaning roles? Is it revenge, a way of giving one's disparagers yet more of what, apparently, they find so distasteful? Is it partly fear, as in, "This role I've been cast in, however ugly, I know I can play, having been seen playing it; other roles are possibly beyond me"? Pure self-hatred? I am guessing all of these destructive factors can be involved.)

And possibly, in this age of social media, the tendency to know oneself only by reflection in the eyes of others is, if anything, only getting worse. I think of the emphasis now placed on being "friended" online.

Since language plays a major part in self-definition—and since grammar shapes language—grammar has a role to play in overriding and undoing the negative perceptions of us that arise communally, then begin to take up lodging deep inside ourselves, where they have the power to do damage in our lives.

Man Being Strangled by a Giant Paragraph,
by George Grosz (courtesy, the Estate of George Grosz)

Distinguishing How You're Perceived from Who You Are

Modeling the I-Statement

ecades ago, psychologists who led therapy groups introduced what still seems to me a powerful linguistic means to keep people from confusing their reactions to each other with the truth about one another. That means was I-statements. Rather than letting one group participant say to a second one, "You're a threatening woman," they required all participants to refrain from definitional character assassination and to confine themselves, instead, to reports of their own feelings. "You're threatening" became "I feel threatened by you."

Generally speaking, we don't know enough about each other to sum each other up. In general, we do better saying how the other person affects us. With I-statements,

You like putting people down, Bob.

gives way to

In that meeting we just had, I felt belittled by you, Bob.

and the you-statement

Sandra, you are one obsessive micromanager.

is supplanted by

Sandra, I feel I need more discretion in this project than you've given me so far.

Books on raising children, such as Thomas Gordon's *P.E.T. [Parent Effectiveness Training] in Action*, contain many good examples. There, in the mouth of a man whose four-year-old daughter doesn't understand how their play together has exhausted him, the exasperated you-line (slightly tweaked by me)

You stop being a pest now, Iris.

becomes the infinitely kinder I-line

Hey, kid, I'm just too wiped out to play more with you now, okay?

I can tell you this much: Whenever I have found myself on the receiving end of a reductive you-statement, it's triggered my defenses and transformed me into someone quite unpleasant, concealing the authentic, more complex me for a while. To that extent at least, my self-appointed critic succeeds in making me and his portrayal of me into one and the same thing—which, of course, rankles.

Unfortunately, though, we can't simply dictate what types of expression get addressed to us. The undemeaning I-statements that, ideally, would come *our* way are not ours to make.

What we can do is:

- model the alternative ourselves
- diminish (if not ever quite eliminate) the ill effects of others pigeonholing us by noticing what they are doing
- every now and then, take opportunities to call our accusers' attention to their definitional habits of speech, and let them know we don't believe they do us justice.

Other False Equations

Using E-Prime . . . in the Past Tense

The little word "is" has its tragedies: it names and equates different things with the greatest innocence; and yet no two are ever identical.

— GEORGE SANTAYANA

Certain words and phrases correspond to signs in arithmetic. *And* is so akin to *plus* that millions of people can be heard to say, "Two and three make five." *Without, unless,* and phrases like *except for* serve pretty much the role of a minus sign. All forms of the verb *to be*—such as *am, is, are, was, were, has been,* and *will be*—function like an equal sign.

Perhaps this is why it took a would-be scientist, Count Alfred Korzybski, author of *Science and Sanity,* to lead an attack on *to be,* our main copulative verb. With a scientific zeal for precision, he pointed out that no phenomenon "equals" another. At least at the molecular level—and usually at the visible level, too—each contains pieces and aspects to be found nowhere else; each is complicated, each unique. Apple A can't be perfectly equated with Apple B.

Nor can Apple A, as I would describe it at this moment, even be equated with the thing which it's in process to become. In Korzybski's words, a freshly picked apple "may be a very appetizing affair," but on some future date it will present as an "un-edible wet splash." That's how dramatic a flux envelops us.

And if use of *to be* raises problems in relation to apples, how much more so when applied to creatures like ourselves, who far exceed apples in complexity and unpredictability? As one Buddhist scholar sees it (paraphrasing sacred text):

> . . . the mind is ever-changing, so that any [so-called] "person who annoyed me" is no longer that same person by the time those words are uttered.

Which is to say, the sentence "You are cowardly"—built around the verb *are*, a form of *to be*—is highly problematic. It's too simple, and it lacks respect for its subject's variability; that fellow human being is unlikely either *just* to be a coward or to be one always.

I, in my time, have been told I was: a disappointment, a hero, a progressive, a frightened middle-of-the-roader . . . and a score of other things. Every time a permutation of the verb *to be* was used to describe me, it gave me the distinct, paralyzing sense that my whole true self had been laid bare somehow. In each case, I needed to get rid of the erroneous identity being thrust on me. One such identity might wash off cleanly; remnants of another might, unfortunately, stick and infiltrate my core self-concept for a while.

D. David Bourland, Jr., a disciple of Korzybski, became so convinced of the reductive force of all forms of *to be* that in 1965 he began to promote what he called E-Prime, the English language stripped of *be, been, am, are, is, was,* and *were.* (The "E" in "E-Prime" stands for English. "Prime" indicates a variant.) He and associates like E. W. Kellogg III modeled it themselves, in speech as well as writing.

I invite my reader to gauge the difference E-Prime makes. It is one thing to tell oneself,

> I am a landlord now.

quite another to say,

> I own a two-family house now and supplement my income with rent from it.

In E-Prime, the definitional

> I'm such a jerk with women.

gets recycled as the factual

> I just went and treated that girl rudely.

The latter can be lived down, apologized for, survived, and put behind, as the speaker's personality goes on developing.

A proper discussion of E-Prime would take more space than I have here. It has yet to be adopted by more than a handful of speakers and writers, and, to my mind, not all of its effects are as salutary as the one I've highlighted, the elimination of pernicious self-equations. (For example, it can make the use of passive constructions difficult, if not impossible.) Still, its value can hardly be doubted. The college basketball player who, after a loss, is taunted by a gloating fan of the opposing team saying, "Hey there! Thomason! You're not much of an athlete, are you?" should reject definition and stick to the facts, especially in her own head, saying,

> I had trouble at the free throw line today.

or

> For a second time this season, I allowed the
> ball to be stripped away from me.

And that player should, if possible, leave it at that—remain a free agent, so to speak, and turn to other things.

A FURTHER NOTE

My reader may have noticed that in offering alternatives to *to be* verbs, above, I somewhat favor the past tense, as in "went and treated," "had trouble," and "allowed." My first discovery in trying out E-Prime was that, in itself, it doesn't always solve the problem of verbal entrapment. We who care about our freedom from the definitional perceptions others have of us need to watch our tenses also.

Consider the difference between past tense—"I had trouble at the free throw line"—and present tense—"I have trouble at the free throw line." For all the good E-Prime does here, the resigned player who says "I *have* trouble . . . " may as well drop E-Prime altogether and revert to the verb *to be*, saying, "I am someone who's no good at free throws."

What we term the present tense in grammar should usually be called the *present ongoing*. The actual present, that thin line dividing past from future, can't be rendered in words; any utterance attempting to describe it—even a play-by-play broadcast—is out of date by the time one hears the first syllable. While a commentator on the radio is saying that LeBron James "rebounds it and slam-dunks," a member of the other team already has possession of the basketball and can be seen readying to throw it into play from the sidelines.

And outside of running coverage like that, present-tense verbs normally describe actions and conditions that persist; they aren't out of date as soon as one begins to vocalize them. An example would be, "I live in Cambridge." This statement is true both when I speak it and for the foreseeable future.

Thus the basketball player who, in present tense, confesses, "I allow the ball to be stripped away" veers too close to saying, "I am someone who, as an ongoing feature of my identity, allows the ball to be stripped away."

To steer clear of such an effect requires the use of an available *past* tense—simple past tense, as in

I *allowed* the ball to be stripped away.

or past imperfect tense, as in

> I *was allowing* the ball to be stripped away.

or past perfect tense, as in

> I *had allowed* the ball . . . .

Even the present imperfect tense conveys more potential for change than the present tense does:

> I've *been allowing* the ball . . . .

Compare for yourself:

> I smoke two packs a day.

> I've been smoking two packs a day since November, when my husband died.

. . . .

> I run on at the mouth.

> At the events last week, I did too much chattering, now that I think of it.

What's past is past.

The Linguistic Limits to Freedom

Our Names

She called herself Lil
But everyone knew her as Nancy.

— THE BEATLES

When I began this book, I never imagined dwelling for so long on the topic of freedom. I had not yet looked around and noted all the features of language that effectively keep us in our places, unchanged.

Possibly the subtlest enforcer of the status quo is our use of proper nouns—that is, names.

Because I have a name, I have a reputation that precedes me. On the campus where I taught for decades, a veteran colleague of mine might well tell a new department member, "You should see Larry Weinstein about your idea; that's *his* kind of thing" (or, in hushed tones, "Whatever you do, don't float ideas like that in Larry Weinstein's hearing"). My name has functioned in the way a brand name does: It assures the world at large of what to expect from me, the named product; it commodifies me.

In ways imperceptible to us, we feel constrained by our names. One of the reasons we take vacations is to be among people who don't know us by name and won't be shocked if suddenly we act out of character.

What can be done about names, though? We need our names.

When it comes to personal identity being stuck in place—identity as broken record—I'm hard put to formulate a good, comprehensive verbal cure. All I can propose is those maneuvers discussed in the preceding essays:

- I-statements (insofar as we can manage to get others to transmit their feedback to us *in* I-statements)
- E-Prime
- and the past tense.

They are, I hope, enough at least to keep the soil of one's personality loose and arable, a terrain still able to support new growth.

Near the end of a prayer known as the Amidah, Jews ask God to help them respond to their enemies—those who call Jews *names*—by letting their own souls "be as dust" toward their detractors. And the Hebrew word for "dust" (*ahfar*) is the same word used in Genesis: "Then the Lord God formed man of the dust of the ground." It's the vital stuff of which we're made. If the writers of the prayer had only meant to say that one should be silent in the face of demeaning misrepresentation, they might have resorted to the simile of stone, but they did not. Wisely, I would say, they chose a simile not for ossified, inanimate silence but for life's very source. The appropriate response for a victim of name-calling is not to stand stock still and thereby cooperate in his own diminution like a stone, but to recall his ultimately true state, unnameability, and go on evolving.

Having One's Own Way of Seeing

"Actually," the Set-Up-and-Reject Formula

Whoever fills his life only with what's good and beautiful in the eyes of others—he is a slave.
— RAV KOOK

There's another type of freedom-from-community worth striving for, with grammar's help: freedom of thought. It's the opposite of groupthink.

My former longtime colleague David Honick once told me of the fellow graduate student who, fifty years before, had had a study carrel—an assigned desk and shelves—next to his in Harvard's huge Widener Library. David's own carrel was plentifully stocked with books he was consulting for his dissertation, but his neighbor's was empty, a student's bare cupboard, and the neighbor himself arrived there with only a blank lined yellow pad in hand, where he'd write thoughts down, apparently out of the blue. When, eventually, David asked his name, the mysterious abutter replied, "Noam Chomsky." He would go on to become the most influential linguist of our times.

A person's decision to rely heavily on books (or other sources of authority) for getting at the truth of matters often amounts to the decision to let others relieve her of the work it would entail to do brave thinking on her own. As much as we may prize freedom, we are all members of a species much given to laziness and fear, who frequently seek cover in what passes for the truth among our peers, or throughout society in our times. On topics ranging from the way a mutual friend has been dressing lately to the merits of a current bestseller, we must be on guard against becoming mere mouthpieces for the views of others.

Slavish echoing is a behavior familiar to us from childhood. We all engaged in it as toddlers and preschoolers. Who has not observed the child three or four years old as she converses with a doll in words taken from the lips of her own mother? She pulls a nice knit hat off the doll's head and says, "This is for the baby, not for you— babies' heads get cold, because they don't have hair." Or she reassures her doll with sentences that start, "When you grow up . . . ."

The Swiss psychologist Jean Piaget, who spent thousands of hours transcribing and studying children's utterances, concluded that preschoolers do not always draw a line between others' words and their own, but often experience all words in their consciousness *as* their own.

... [This type of] imitation would seem to be . . . a confusion between the I and the not-I . . . .

. . . The child does not know that he is imitating . . . . This is why children up to the age of six or seven, when they have had something explained to them and are asked to do it immediately afterwards, invariably imagine that they have discovered by them-selves what in reality they are only repeating from a model.

By and by, of course, we're expected to distinguish between our own thoughts and the beliefs of others, but telling where the boundary is can be devilishly hard to do—even at the age of seventy—for someone who has not yet come *into* his own, sensing and inhabiting his unique consciousness.

Ernest Hemingway reported that his greatest difficulty as a writer was "knowing what you really felt, rather than what you were supposed to feel, or what you had been taught to feel." Had Hemingway lived somewhat longer, he would have appreciated Woody Allen's invention of a vaudeville routine that featured the parrot who could sing "I Gotta Be Me."

How, then, to keep things honest, short of doing our thinking at the South Pole, or at a solitary study carrel, stripped of others' words and thoughts?

One expedient I've used is what I call *adverbial disclosers*:

> To be honest with you
> I have to say
> Actually
> Despite what you might well suppose my
>   feelings on this subject to be
> Though I hate to stand out as an oddball
> I wish I could I agree with you, but
> Off the record . . . .

An introductory word or phrase of this sort (if it hasn't yet become a glib, formulaic add-on with me) performs the function of a sharp linoleum knife: It gives me a purchase on a layer of my thought further down than my first, socially conditioned—that is, derivative—response to a question, *staking* me to that (for me) truer depth. I can then dispense with second-hand thought, lifting it and stripping it away as I go.

By this grammatical stratagem, I come that much closer to saying what *I* have to say.

And the habit of tracking my true feelings then stays operative in me in diverse settings. If, for example, the street performer that I pass downtown while doing errands is producing sweeter tunes than I have heard on Pandora or my car radio, I don't let the fact that he is not an object of popular excitement keep me from noticing how much I'm enjoying his sound or from scribbling his name on one of my packages. (This might be a good time for my reader to stop briefly and listen to the Joni Mitchell song "Real Good for Free.")

I hope not to walk through life and praise just those smells pre-*advertised* as fragrant—that is, the roses. If, for instance, a specific, unadulterated odor of my body pleases me, I hope to be able to say so, at least to good friends, in the spirit of Walt Whitman, who declared,

> The scent of these armpits is aroma finer
> than prayer . . . .

As the poet Delmore Schwartz once said, in discussing existentialism, nobody "can take a bath *for* you." I would like to be "all there" when my life happens, and to let it register in all its real-time truth on my five senses, however much that felt-experience deviates from the prejudgments of society-at-large.

Probably it goes without saying, but the effects of prejudging—a synonym for which is prejudice—can do more damage than pedestrians' reflexive dismissal of a street performer's music does. Society's prejudgment of armpit smell didn't cost Walt Whitman much, but its strongly biased views of same-sex love may well have cost him dearly.

In my own case, it's society's demeaning preconceptions of old age that have recently come into play. An outstanding school announced an opportunity for practicing playwrights that enticed me instantly. I went to the website for it and filled out most of an application form there before coming to a drop-down menu for entering my age. It stopped at fifty-nine, several years shy of my tenancy on Earth to that date. I couldn't help but think, "Fifty-nine?! I've learned *crucial* things about my craft since then. It would have been more sensible to *start* the menu at age fifty-nine!"

I have yet to write my protest about this to the co-directors of the theater program. When I do, I might call on one of the disclosers listed above, like *actually*—

> **Actually**, from where I sit, not only have my powers as a playwright not waned since I turned 60, they have grown.

Or I might set my letter up with what I call a set-up-and-reject formula, which begins by laying out a false belief and ends by debunking it:

> **I should not have been surprised, I know, that** in a country where the insights and new intuitions that come with age have always been devalued, even seasoned theater pros like the two of you might be skeptical of people "just coming up" in their craft in the sixth or seventh decade of life. **That said, however,** . . . . [And, of course, here the other shoe would start to drop.]

Other set-up-and-reject phrases I could use include

> **Yes, the common wisdom is** that, by age 60, one has already revealed whatever gifts one has. **That claim, though, is belied** by true stories of aging "baby boomers."

Many authors have observed what harm results when people silently adopt prejudices in the social air surrounding them—even buying into ones targeting the very groups which they themselves belong to. No one writing on the subject has been more eloquent than Martin Luther King, who said, "Our lives begin to end the day we become silent about things that matter." He was not referring to the biological last phase of life, but to the end (at any age) of engaged life, a transition marked by giving up the effort to use language to call out falsehood.

Friends in the Graveyard

A Special Use of Present Tense

The dead who think
And live in ink.
— FROM AN UNPUBLISHED POEM BY
WARREN WEINSTEIN

When, some few years ago, I had my first excruciating episode with a kidney stone, Warren, my brother and a lover of books, told me to reread Montaigne's essay on kidney stones, which I did. The sympathy of family and friends, though conveyed in real time by moving lips, paled next to the consolation provided by the written words of the world's first essayist. Of all my comforters, only this man born in 1533 had had stones himself. Only he, for example, knew of the unusual euphoria that instantly envelops the sufferer on passing a stone.

I used my ad hoc consultation with Montaigne about our shared medical condition as an excuse to reacquaint myself with other pieces of his thought, ranging from perhaps the first influential call for religious tolerance in Christian Europe to a lawyerly defense of men's "male member," which opens with the concession,

> We are right in remarking the untamed liberty of this member. He puffs himself up most importunely when we do not need him, and swoons away when our need is greatest.

As a result, phenomenologically speaking, Montaigne once again became a closer, more audible presence in my life than most of my contemporaries. In the words Montaigne himself uses about Tacitus, the Roman historian whose pronouncements still applied in Montaigne's own time, "You might often think that he was pinching me."

Some writers have lodged not only their ideas but bits of their actual text in my head, so that on relevant occasions—ones demonstrating their old, well-turned words' enduring applicability—they are practically the first things out of my mouth. When I enter a new, beautifully designed workplace, home, or church, I frequently find myself quoting Hannah Arendt's "No activity can become excellent if the world does not provide a proper space for its exercise." When, in autumn, I first notice dried leaves flying in confusion up the pavement in front of me, I privately recite Shelley's phrase in "Ode to the West Wind": "like ghosts from an enchanter fleeing." If I had no recourse to Montaigne, Shelley, Arendt, or a thousand other legally deceased persons—for their rare insights, as well as for their keen sense perceptions—I would feel an even deeper isolation from my true condition than I do in this strange world.

Others appear to have used books as I do. I think of the Cuban workers who rolled cigars to the sound of a paid lector reading from great books—a practice of the late nineteenth and early twentieth centuries dramatized by Nilo Cruz in his play *Anna in the Tropics* (where the Anna mentioned is Anna Karenina, whose story is the story being read to the workers). I think of the subway commuter who shuts me and our fellow travelers out of his consciousness in order to absorb ten pages of Camus.

Also, I think of Malcolm X's awakening to books at the Norfolk Prison Colony, of which experience he writes, "Up to then, I never had been free . . . ," and of all the closeted gay readers in the last century who stumbled on these lines by C. P. Cavafy:

> Later . . . in a more perfect society . . .
> someone else made just like me
> is certain to appear and act freely.

The emperor Marcus Aurelius is said to have attended gladiatorial combat only out of duty, since he abhorred its brutality. Reportedly, he brought books with him to read there, in plain view of the crowd. I, in my turn, read Aurelius, as the world goes on (and, in fact, goes on going *awry* in some major respects) around me.

We need means to induce such spirits to stay with us, revivify us, buoy us up. Is there any verbal method for expanding one's community to include past residents of Earth? Yes, although the one our language has to offer for the purpose looks small.

In English, we accommodate the need for ancestral companionship only to the extent that we permit use of present-tense verbs in reporting words or thoughts found in writerly texts—novels, poems, plays, treatises, and so on—even if their authors have returned to dust. We say,

> In *An Ideal Husband,* Oscar Wilde skewers . . . .

or, again in present tense,

> Melville's Captain Ahab is obsessed with . . . .

English stingily withholds such life-in-perpetuity from *spoken* words, even if they have great significance. We don't say, using present tense,

> In her testimony at the House Committee on Un-American Activities, Lillian Hellman declares, "I cannot and will not cut my conscience to fit this year's fashions."

We say,

> . . . Hellman declared . . . .

And we don't say,

> My late Grandma Hlady tells me never to forget about the folks who don't grow up with advantages like I have.

We say,

> Grandma Hlady told me . . . .

Why not do what other things we can, though, to clear channels between us and those voices in the cemetery that still merit having true immediacy in our lives? Let's put Grandma's words between quotation marks, then situate them in a verbal formula that makes our repetition of them in the present tense acceptable. Let's say—to ourselves, at least, and right out loud, when appropriate—"I can still hear Grandma telling me . . . ."

GRAMMAR FOR MORALE

Where the essays in the preceding section offer grammatical help for countering others' distortions of oneself, the following two essays offer help from grammar for dealing with true personal failure.

We need ways to maintain positive self-regard even as exhibits A, B, C, D, and E mount against us in the inner courtroom and we fear that more such proof of our incompetence is in transit there.

Fulcrum

"But"

In the months following his graduation from Bentley University, a student of mine from China had several setbacks to his career. When I asked him how he was doing, he responded by telling me the story of General Zeng Guofan, who, in despair about the progress of a war, had drafted a report to the emperor reading,

> We fight, but the enemy defeats us.

When his protégé, General Zuo, read Zeng's draft, he proposed revising it to read,

> The enemy defeats us, but we fight on.

According to my student, the revised text reassured Zeng's ruler and enabled Zeng himself to remain in good spirits.

We are faced throughout our days with this grammatical decision: the choice of what to put before the conjunction *but* and what to put after it. Whatever goes last usually receives emphasis (called by grammarians *end-focus*).

The choice is ours alone to make: Our community asks only that both claims—the one that precedes *but* and the one that follows it—be basically true, to our best knowledge. By filling in the *but* clause, we exercise the astounding power to declare which truth is the proper takeaway—the more useful of the two, going forward—and no one dare object.

Take, for instance, the quite deft and heart-sustaining use of *but* in two places in this quote of Edward Everett Hale:

> I am only one, but I am still one.
> I cannot do everything, but still I can do
>   something.
> And just because I cannot do everything, I
>   will not refuse to do the
> something that I can do.

But, then, is a charmed fulcrum: Put an army to its left in your sentence, a feather to its right, and magically the feather will outweigh the troops. The power manifest in saying what goes left and right of *but* is, no doubt, part of what John Milton meant when he described the mind as making "a Heav'n of Hell, a Hell of Heav'n."

Over the past five years of being a widower, I have had to tell myself, "Yes, my adored life-partner of some forty-five years is absolutely gone now . . . but life itself goes on." If I had reversed the order of my two truths (try *starting off* my sentence with "Yes, life goes on, but . . . "), I might never have been able to resume the work in life that's my calling or to find a new, wonderful companion for the years left to me.

Despair could have stopped me in my tracks or turned me into unattractive company for others.

I used to ridicule the insistent, upbeat tone of Norman Vincent Peale's *The Power of Positive Thinking*. These days, not so much. Now, on rereading, I seem to notice more nuance in it. For one thing, Peale does not deny that life mixes good and bad, but asserts only that it's " . . . better to emphasize the good, [since], as you do that, good seems to increase." And most of the instances he cites to support this conviction ring true to me. I have little trouble, for example, believing him about the laid-off worker who interviews poorly for new jobs until he sheds the bitterness engulfing him about his old one. "Yes," I tell myself as I read Peale, "nothing which this worker could do is likelier to move him on to brighter times than to reconstruct the language he uses to describe his circumstances." Overall, I now see, Peale qualifies as a reliable witness in the cause of *but*.

And then there is the feeling of having been laid-off not by some mere foreman but by God—that is, of being damaged goods on Earth in *moral* terms.

Peale, a minister of the Reformed Church in America, no doubt drew his thinking from a long and beautiful Christian tradition of belief in grace, the availability of full redemption at whatever hour it is sought. As the thirteenth century figure Meister Eckhart writes,

> But if a man rises completely above sin and turns away from it . . . God acts as if the sinner hadn't even sinned once. He will not allow that man to suffer for one moment . . . .

Jews like myself have thinkers of a similar persuasion to consult when moral bearings get misplaced and the soul begins to feel contaminated. One is the eighteenth century Hasidic master Nachman of Bratzlav, in whose collection of works, *Likutey Moharan*, one finds a teaching called "Azamra," or "I Will Sing" (Psalm 146):

> When you start looking deep inside your-self, you may think you have no good in you at all . . . . Don't let yourself fall into depression. Search until you find some little good in you. How could it be that you never did anything good in your whole life?

> When you start examining your good deed, you may see that it had flaws. Maybe you did it for the wrong reasons and with the wrong attitude. Even so, how could your mitzvah [your right act] . . . contain *no* good?
>
> . . . . . .

> In like manner, you must go on finding more and more good points. For this, [you see,] is the way *songs* are made: by sifting the good from the bad . . . .

> A musical instrument is basically a vessel containing air. The musician produces sounds by causing air to vibrate. His task is to move his hands on the instrument in

such a way as to produce *good* spirit, *good* vibration, while avoiding bad vibration—dissonant gloom and depression.

When a person refuses to allow himself to fall into despair but instead gives himself new life by finding and gathering his positive points, he makes melodies. He can then [celebrate].

Mindfully deploying the conjunction *but* is not the one and only grammatical means for bringing oneself back from setbacks. I think especially of *subordinate clauses of concession—*clauses that begin with words like *although* or *despite*, as in

Although, in the end, Rob wanted to stop dating, our one year together showed me I could get to be more intimate with someone than I'd ever thought was possible in my case.

The subordinate clause here (beginning with "Although . . . ") houses the part of the story which the speaker wants to downplay. She correctly saves her main clause for the part she'd like to feature and dwell upon now.

If we're not to lose heart in the aftermath of failures, we must take care how we tell our stories. (At least one current tack among psychologists—narrative therapy—makes the apt revision of demoralizing self-talk about one's past its chief aim.) In his mind, the bankrupt entrepreneur can foreground either (a) the mistakes he made that led to bankruptcy or

(b) what success he had enjoyed for a while and the marketable skills he acquired as a result of it all. He must learn to say, "In the end, yes, I went belly up, *but* . . . ."

Grammar, Thing of Beauty

Sentence Length and Repetition, among Other Things

Don't hide your light under a bushel.
— Proverb based on the Gospel
of Luke, 8:16–18

God gives us each a song.
— A Saying of the Ute Indians

What can do more to enhance a person's sense of self than exercising the ability to bring new beautiful things into the world, such as vibrant paintings or expressive tunes?

Another in this book's long list of surprises about grammar is that, like art and music, it lends itself to the creation of beauty. As Joan Didion once said, "Grammar is a piano I play by ear."

At its aesthetic best, a sentence's grammar in some way mimics the content of what is being said. For example, to evoke the suddenness of my realization that something unusual was taking place before me, I might put off naming what it was until the end of my sentence and then spring it on my reader just as suddenly as it was sprung on me. I might write,

> There, out of airy nowhere, in perfect silence
> at my feet, an interminable line of capable
> black ants was invading the house.

The possibilities for imitative beauty through grammar could fill volumes, as I hope the published specimens below will suggest.

In the description of a phone call that opens her essay "The Cult of Busyness," Barbara Ehrenreich recounts all of the news that a harried friend of hers has used the call to unload on her. Ehrenreich does so in a rapid-fire series of unelaborated clauses that produces the grammatical equivalent of her friend's harried-ness. By contrast, Ehrenreich's description of her own laid-back "activity" during that same phone call—touching her toes—is fittingly set forth in leisurely detail and capped by a slow, gratuitous appositive (the phrase beginning "a pastime"):

> Not too long ago a former friend and soon-
> to-be acquaintance called me up to tell me
> how busy she was. A major report, upon
> which her professional future depended, was
> due in three days; her secretary was on strike;
> her housekeeper had fallen into the hands of

the Immigration Department; she had two hours to prepare a dinner party for eight; and she was late for her time-management class. Stress was taking its toll, she told me: her children resented the fact that she sometimes got their names mixed up, and she had taken to abusing white wine.

All this put me at a distinct disadvantage, since the only thing I was doing at the time was holding the phone with one hand and attempting to touch the opposite toe with the other hand, a pastime that I had perfected during previous telephone monologues.

Of the Southdale Mall in Minnesota—the first indoor shopping mall, now more than fifty years old—Malcolm Gladwell writes, "It does not seem like a historic building, which is precisely why it is one." And to make his point that all other such malls, even the newest, are copies of that one, he goes on to use the bold grammatical device of simple repetition:

> Fifty years ago, Victor Gruen designed a fully enclosed, introverted, multitiered, double-anchor-tenant shopping complex with a garden court under a skylight—and today virtually every regional shopping center in America is a fully enclosed, introverted, multitiered, double-anchor-tenant complex with a garden court under a skylight.

To convey how rapidly a comrade in the Vietnam War went from being bright and strong to being dull and crippled, Richard Currey deploys at least three grammatical devices: He sticks mostly to relentless, relatively short, direct sentences. He writes all but one of them in the present tense, even though the change being described took weeks or months to run its course. And he disallows pausing by dispensing with paragraph breaks. By the end, we're made to feel what Currey himself feels, that his friend's awful transformation occurred in no time at all.

Miguel Maldonado is nineteen years of age, a Lance Corporal in the United States Marine Corps, a first-generation Cuban-American from Miami, Florida. He is smart, funny, courageous . . . . He has, on more than one occasion, saved the lives of his fellow marines and platoon commander. He gets on with everybody in his unit, no matter their backgrounds, prejudices, religion, or politics. He has a natural inclination toward excellence: a soldier's soldier. He speaks of a career in the Marine Corps, telling everyone he has found a home at last. He is astonished to find himself successful and, despite the stress of combat, he is a happy man. It is in the last days of 1968 that, [with me nearby], Maldonado loses his right leg at mid-thigh and I use his belt as a crude tourniquet in the

minutes before he is airlifted to the Naval
Hospital at Cam Ranh Bay. When I see him
next it is by chance, having escorted two
wounded marines into the same hospital.
There has been some trouble with the
leg—a sloppy amputation, an infection—and
Maldonado is medically addicted to opiates
of one form or another. The bright energy
and wide-eyed courage are gone. Maldonado
knows that he has entered the next stage of
his life: a disabled high-school dropout drug
addict, without prospects or direction.

Does Currey's disheartening content disqualify this
passage from consideration for beauty? Not in my view.
Perhaps beauty's most important function is one that playwright Arthur Miller named: "to take [one's] agony home
and teach it to sing." Showing care in the expression of what's
awful in our lives renders it a bit more bearable somehow.

The discredited but gifted author James Frey simulates
how barriers came down between himself and his parents
when they paid a visit to him at a drug rehab facility. He
produces that effect by removing normal barriers between
sentences and by willfully conflating the singular *each of us*
with the plural *we*:

We pull each of us pulls and we hug each other
the three of us hug each other it is strong and
easy and full of something maybe love.

For a last example, I return to a piece by Annie Dillard that I quoted from earlier in this book. By varying the length of whole sentences in that piece, Dillard carries us aloft with a remarkable bird she spots—a bird that imitates the stunt pilots at an air show. She begins,

> The show was over. It was late.

That is, a sentence of just four words is followed by an even more abrupt sentence, as much to say, "Closing time. Everybody out." But then, in keeping with her subject (a bird's soaring flight), the number of her words per sentence soars.

> Just as I turned from the runway, something caught my eye. It was a swallow, incredibly having its own air show, apparently inspired by stunt pilot Rahm. It climbed way up high over the runway, held its wings oddly, tipped them, and then rolled down the air in loops, winning a spontaneous laugh from me as it performed.

(I have tweaked Dillard's prose a bit here, to make the effect more pronounced.)

Jimi Hendrix found potential for expressive beauty in feedback from his amp. (I think in particular of his "Star Spangled Banner," with its eerily whistling "bombs bursting in air.") Hip-hop artists found the same in the sound of a needle scratching vinyl. Should we expect any less from a storehouse of devices as rich and vast as grammar?

Much as loop-de-loops and nosedives lit a fire under Annie Dillard's swallow, the maneuvers of writers like Dillard can, in turn, inspire us, their readers, to attempt new feats of spirit.

GRAMMAR FOR MINDFULNESS

The most sacred utterance in Jewish liturgy is Deuteronomy 6:4, the Shema. It begins,

> Hear, O Israel: the Lord our
> God, the Lord is One.

It's primarily a call upon the people to listen, to open their ears wide to all that surrounds them and discover the unifying wonder of it all—discover, in religious terms, that a force beyond our reckoning animates the whole of creation.

Did the speaker, Moses, truly think that his enormous crowd at Sinai would be able, at his words, to attune itself to humankind's real situation?

That would have been hard for them. Even in the relatively uniform landscape of a desert, there had to be distractions on all sides, making an experience of "oneness" with reality unlikely. As Moses spoke, there had to be at least a dozen babies crying, a nearly deaf old man loudly asking someone else what Moses was saying, a desert wind that made the tent flaps snap . . . . And those were just the fleeting, small barriers to "hearing."

Sundry larger barriers have always stood between ourselves and a mindful life, a life attuned to hints of our true situation in this *world. If I'm right that any fully realized man or woman is so attuned, we need somehow to get past those obstructions.*

What elements of grammar have a role to play in fostering "attunement"?

Quite a few, I'd say. Certain prior chapters in this book—like the one on passive voice and the one on disclosers ("actually," etc.)—have already dealt with aspects of a mindful life. The chapters in this section of the book take up aspects I have left unmentioned till now because they don't fit neatly under any of my other section headings. Each takes up a different obstacle to mindfulness.

When not using grammar wisely, we

- *overlay reality with a gauze of "spin"— either on the upside with excited hype or on the downside with unfounded fear*
- *buy into the false perception that the world can be owned*
- *forget how ignorant we are, ultimately*
- *shut ourselves off from what transpires around us until we've implemented plans we have.*

Avoiding Hype and Fearfulness

Overuse of Exclamation Marks, Superlatives, Italics, and Intensifiers

> *Human noises vexed the chief god Enlil so much that he persuaded the divine assembly to vote for the destruction of mankind....*
> — *THE ERIDU GENESIS*, CIRCA 1600 B.C.

Many writers and grammarians inveigh against what I might call "typographical overkill," meaning the extensive use of italics, exclamation marks, intensifiers (*really*, *absolutely*, and the like), and glib superlatives (*all-time best* instead of *good*, *worst* instead of *bad*, etc.). They view such devices—when employed too freely—as insults to a reader's intelligence.

Consider this factual description of an enticing dessert, followed by a hyped alternative to it. The original:

The aromatic apple pie had a flaky crust
dusted with cinnamon, many juicy apple
pieces mixed with raisins, and a satisfying
taste of butter to it, too.

The alternative (featuring all four grammatical weapons
of overkill—italics, exclamation marks, intensifiers, and
superlatives) goes,

This incredibly enticing, aromatic apple pie
had everything going for it: It had a *flaky
crust dusted with cinnamon!* It had *countless
juicy apples mixed with raisins!* On top of
which . . . well, just don't get me started on
the unsurpassed way *butter* had been used in
this fabulous creation of a local baker!

Writers who balloon their emphasis with grammar in that
manner may be better-intentioned than the boy who cried
wolf, but they share that boy's fate: Their audience soon opts
to discount them and their words—they would have done
better to let the thing which they describe speak for itself.

Recently, I saw *Three Identical Strangers,* a stellar docu-
mentary film about triplets who were separated after birth
but reunited as adults—but I didn't go because of the ads for
it; I went despite the ads. The ads only blared the following
headline at me:

The Most Amazing, Incredible, Remarkable
True Story Ever Told.

My reaction to hyperbole is much like Lewis Thomas's. Regarding exclamation marks, Thomas writes, "Look! they say, look at what I just said!" When he is subjected to these strident marks, Thomas feels as if he's " . . . being forced to watch someone else's small child jumping up and down crazily in the center of the living room, shouting to attract attention." (Unfortunately, thanks to Thomas and his vivid simile, I now see in every excla- mation mark—in the mark itself, its rigidly vertical form—a rigid six-year-old, arms pressed tight against her sides, trying without success to stand on her dot-like head for all to marvel at.) "If," writes Thomas, "a sentence really has something of impor- tance to say, it doesn't need a mark to point it out."

I myself will use an exclamation mark from time to time— there's a place for it. But I'm likelier to buy a claim if the speaker making it doesn't shriek at me and try to overwhelm me, effectively inserting a barrier of noise between me and apple pie or other things of note.

If you were an employer, which job applicant would you tend to trust more, the one who sends you email reading, "What an awesome pleasure it was to meet you today! The manage- ment position at your store sounds *truly, absolutely perfect for me!*" or the one whose message reads, "It was quite a pleasure meeting you at last. For years, I have been impressed by the caliber of your team—I would be honored to join it. I hope the unusual results I achieved in increasing sales at Macy's and Target make me a candidate worth your considering."

Yet, in many contexts, we give verbal hype free entree to us, letting it fill us with overblown belief in good things to come. When we do, our grasp on reality becomes diffuse and weakens.

That is, the loss of others' trust is not the only price a writer pays when she or he overuses all the orthographic marks and phraseology that smack of gross exaggeration. The cost to mindfulness—by which I mean the cost to our relaxed but keen attentiveness to things—is at least as consequential, for both speaker and listener alike. Regardless of whether my topic is the Taj Mahal or a sale on at the outlet shoe store, using hyperbolic phrases like *the most unbelievable* doesn't help prepare me or my listener to retain and bring along a state of mind for registering what is factual there.

And exaggeration of the dark sort—catastrophizing—is, if anything, doubly problematic: It creates and stokes unnecessary fear.

Imagine that one afternoon, on your way into your house, you find a flyer in the mailbox that reads,

HOMEOWNERS ON THIS STREET! LET OUR RECKLESS CITY COUNCIL HEAR FROM YOU TONIGHT, BEFORE THE VALUE OF YOUR PROPERTY PLUMMETS!

On talk radio and cable TV news, not to mention all the front pages of tabloids for sale at market checkout counters, language of this kind is standard fare now, broadcasting loud alarms to accompany us through the day. ("*Next* up: breaking news about the highly toxic water you've been drinking!")

I grew up with many fears and so, in my adulthood, kept a list of reasons to deny fear its sway over me. Here is what my list came out to be:

1. Fear is unpleasant. (If I let myself become alarmed by news reports of killer bees headed my way from Brazil, it will cloud my enjoyment of time out-of-doors.)

2. Being fearful makes me unpleasant company for others. (Scanning the horizon for bees, I'll become a less attentive host to guests in my backyard.)

3. The events I fear may never occur. (Thanks to climate differences or a new insecticide under development, killer bees may never make it to my region of the U.S.)

4. If what I fear does come to pass—as with that devastating global virus COVID-19—being in a fearful state of mind isn't usually conducive to a good response to it. (It was partly fear of economic hardship that led millions of us to make choices during the pandemic that only prolonged it, so that economic straits—not to mention death and suffering—went to more appalling levels than they would have otherwise.)

5. Being fearful keeps me from taking reasonable risks in the pursuit of worthy goals. (Should I let a mere handful of reportedly deadly bee attacks deter me from

participating in a scientific mission to the Amazon to address environmental problems?)

6. Being fearful is a stressor; it undermines physical health.

We need all the help that we can get to tame our fears, including grammatical help. At the very least, we should adopt a grammar sparing in its use of devices known to be fear triggers.

And there is a large, related matter I need to bring in here: Recourse to our overlay of the intensives, etc.—whether in catastrophizing or in hyping—perpetuates the vast, unexpressed illusion that this world almost *requires* human blustering. It feeds a myth we have bought into that, without all the commotion we produce through jackhammers and our grammar, there might *be* no world; we and our incessant, windy breath are what have kept it in rotation on its axis.

That isn't so, as Mizuta Masahide, a Japanese poet of three centuries ago, intimates in his brief poem that follows. (I take his word *barn* to represent all human artifice obstructing our view of what is real.)

Barn's burnt down.
I can now . . .
See the moon.

Taking Ownership with a Grain of Salt

The Possessive Pronouns

It is easier for a camel to go through the eye of a needle than for a rich man to enter the kingdom of God.

— Gospel of Matthew 19:24

In a classic moment in the history of TV comedy, faint-hearted Jack Benny—whose tight-fisted character never parted with a dollar—is suddenly held up at gunpoint on the street. With a succinctness appropriate to the occasion, the assailant says, "Your money or your life!" All eyes in America then turn to Benny.

At first, he seems to be reacting normally to the event: He is stunned and frightened. Then, however, we commence to notice how distracted Benny looks—and how very long he's taking to reach for his wallet—and it dawns on us: That stock question of the robber might, for our man Benny, not be quite the no-brainer it's been taken for by other victims of a mugging.

When several more seconds have elapsed (and the live TV audience can be heard starting to chuckle knowingly), Benny's hapless thief finally repeats himself with greater urgency—"I said, 'Your money or your life, Bud!'"—and Benny, sure enough, turns on him and whines, "I'm thinking! I'm t.h.i.n.k.i.n.g!!!" (I wish I could replicate in writing Benny's timing and inflection at this long-past TV moment, which ignited laughter from one coast to the other.)

The thief has made a crucial mistake, and it was grammatical.

By employing the possessive pronoun *your*—not just to Benny's life but to his money, too—he has reinforced Benny's deeply mixed-up notion that whatever bills and coins might be sitting in his pocket at the moment are as much a part of him as his flawed heart. Benny's would-be robber might have gotten farther saying, "Okay, Bud, I want the money, or it's your life." *The* money—not *your* money.

There, as best I understand it, is the problem with *your, my, his,* and *hers*: They enforce the ancient legal fiction that the individual alone has rights to what he has amassed of this world's wealth—exclusive rights to all the money on deposit in his name at the bank and to all the items that he puts away in places such as drawers and the garage. They are what God meant for him and no one else.

Ah, but I can sense a thousand political knives being unsheathed at these words of mine. Here may be as good a place as any—in this grammar book—to honestly declare I am not a Communist. Just because I call possession "fiction" doesn't mean I want to see that old, foundational assumption dropped. I may be distressed (which is to say, I am) by the enormous gulf between "haves" and "have-nots" on Earth, but we have seen enough of the disastrous and bloody attempts in the last century to abolish private property. We can justifiably conclude that *Homo sapiens* is probably not made for comprehensive pooling of the world's resources beyond that represented by our roads, public schools and libraries, safety nets to guarantee good basic services to all the old and sick among us, and similar essential holdings-in-common.

What is more, the grammatical/legal fiction of ownership has yielded many in the world—certainly me and a number of my friends—a measure of true affluence. As Adam Smith, the primary theorist of capitalism, taught us more than two hundred years ago, personal greed—when relatively unfettered by laws and tariffs—can, with time, raise the standard of living enjoyed by the greediest and the least greedy alike (although, increasingly, the evidence suggests that wise regulation and a labor movement in good trim make the "trickle-down" effect run more smoothly). Without there being well-established rights to personal property, the gears of Smith's benevolent machine would never have begun to turn. Much of what we value in the physical world— from indoor plumbing and cars to winter getaways in the Caribbean (and, for that matter, almost all the books on my shelves)—would either not exist or not be within the means of a majority of people.

No, I have no intention of taking to the street with placards for the abolition of private property. For reasons of the spirit, though, we need to recall that the world is not ultimately ownable by us. We had no hand in its creation—in fact, for all of our pretensions, the biggest of us are but small, time-limited visitors to Earth; it ought to be a daily wonder to us.

When we don't take care, the possessive mindset—*my*, *your*, *his* and so forth—casts a thick, misleading veil over all things.

On occasions when I can detect our deep confusion about ownership, I like to return to Henry David Thoreau's writings. In *Walden*, referring to a farm legally owned by someone else, Thoreau memorably claims to have "retained" its landscape for himself and, in so doing, to have "carried off" the wealth it represented.

The speaker in the Robert Frost poem "Stopping by Woods on a Snowy Evening" would seem to be venturing into the same transgressive psychic space occupied by Thoreau, though more guardedly. He opens with a short acknowledgment of the rights of property—"Whose woods these are I think I know"—but then proceeds to take the scene before him in with all the same free pleasure thought to be the legal owner's right alone. That scene is "lovely, dark and deep," he says.

I have found it hard to come up with good language for elaborating on the Thoreau-Frost perception here, which transcends our legal, mundane way of apportioning the world. Let me let Thoreau speak for me, then. In the essay "Walking," he entertains two possible derivations of the word "saunter."

> I have met with but one or two persons in the
> course of my life who understood the art of

> Walking, that is, of taking walks—who had
> a genius, so to speak, for *sauntering,* which
> word is beautifully derived "from idle people
> who roved about the country, in the Middle
> Ages, and asked charity, under pretense of
> going [in the French] *a la Sainte Terre,*" to
> the Holy Land, till the children exclaimed,
> "There goes a *Sainte-Terrer,*" a Saunterer,
> a Holy-Lander . . . . Some, however, would
> derive the word from *sans terre,* without
> land or a home, which, in the good sense,
> will mean having no particular home but
> [being] equally at home everywhere. For
> this is the secret of successful sauntering.

Thoreau's way of tying sacredness to dispossession reso-
nates deeply with me. Inheritance and personal earnings—in
beneficially securing for us *special* rights to *certain* things—
simultaneously limit our appreciation for the given world in
its miraculous totality.

What happens if we . . . oh, not disown ownership, but
downgrade it, by declining to employ the genitive case—*my,*
your, and the rest—on at least some of the occasions when,
through force of habit, it comes automatically to us? What
effect, if any, does it have on mental health to retreat a bit
grammatically from our presumed possession of the world,
by replacing "my chair" every now and then with "the chair
I like to sit in in the evening," or "my new Toyota" with "the
Toyota I've been driving for two years"?

Other possibilities include occasional replacement of

- "my clothes" with "the clothes you see on me at work"
- "my house" with "the house where I live"
- "my company" with "the company I started thirty years ago, and go on running."

I encourage you to try a few such re-phrasings out loud. On me at least, the effect is salutary. I feel a bit less encumbered, and a wee bit less invested in the concept—property—that associates myself with certain objects but blinds me both to them (in their truest nature) and to marvels on all sides.

A song in the Hasidic tradition goes, "How obscure the world remains to all who want it for their own; how illuminating, though, to those who don't."

Uncertainty

Swapping Our Rhetorical Questions for Real Ones; the Ignorant "I"

Are you still capable of knowing nothing?

— Lao Tze

I was once acquainted with a teacher who would boast, "I never ask a question I don't know the answer to."

My big fear about this seasoned influencer of the young was that she self-reported accurately. I found it uncomfortably too easy to imagine her allowing children to regard all questions as mere prompts in a didactic game of guessing at the facts their knowledgeable elders want to hear from them. Such a game may have its place when there is material that needs to be memorized, like twenty crucial dates in German history or the periodic table of elements, but it shouldn't be the way of things all day long.

The need for *open-ended* questioning—whose starting point is an awareness of collective ignorance—pertains at school, at work, in the out-of-doors, at home . . . in a word, everywhere. At stake are not only the advances we crave, like a cure for cancer, but personal mindfulness, as well.

I have worked in settings where it was safe, even praiseworthy, to raise true, open questions about how our team pursued its aims, and I have worked in settings where a person's asking good questions marked her as disloyal, as unfit to be kept on, let alone promoted—settings where, to borrow words from Donald Schön's *The Reflective Practitioner*, " . . . uncertainty is a threat; its admission is a sign of weakness." In the latter, I participated in the tacit shared effort to conceal misgivings and doubts, letting myself fill with cynicism rather than risk losing my paycheck.

The closest things to real questions to be found in such places are rhetorical questions like

> And what can be *done* about delays in delivery? Nothing.

—and false interrogative tags like that at the end of

> We've already wasted time *enough* on old McConnell's off-the-wall proposal, right?

Neither of these is an invitation to engaged response. Each is just a cue for the display of acquiescence.

In such settings, I and my employer both suffered: I, as I've said, learned to be inauthentic. The company, in turn, produced an inferior product. Why inferior? As students of cognition such as Abigail Lipson have discovered, good thought often depends on more than intelligence: It depends on how long thinkers can endure not yet having reached a satisfactory endpoint to their inquiry.

We pay mightily for premature closure on important questions—not just at work, but also in our families, where a person's psychic needs either get noticed and broached or go unmet, and that person's prospects for happiness in life brighten or fade accordingly. Just as, at work, we are hard put to decide how to position our company's new decongestant in the face of an unscrupulous market rival's highly convincing public lies about it, so, too, at home, we struggle with how best to help a son deal with his bullying tormentors down the street. In both cases, our first solutions are likely to be off; sticking to them could yield damaging outcomes.

Besides which, there are all the many unresolved questions that society in general must grapple with, like

> In this budding age of genetic engineering, at what point might predetermining a child's traits go too far? (Would rearranging DNA to guarantee one's progeny a leg up in competitive events like college admissions and mating not be justifiable? If not, why, exactly?)

Certain questions that we have (but rarely say out loud) are so big we call them cosmological, like

How could time ever have started? That is, if
it ever started, wouldn't there have had to be
a *"before* the start"—and doesn't that imply
there was time then, too?

And then there is the greatest unknown of all:

What does the created universe, including
but not limited to humankind, amount to in
the end, in terms of significance?

Fittingly, since grammar is my subject in this book, Saint
Augustine employs a grammatical simile to put across the
impossibility of answering this last question. Augustine (I
paraphrase him loosely) invites us each to picture him- or
herself as a fleeting single word in a sentence that runs on for
countless miles. Each of us makes the brief appearance we're
allotted in that possibly unending sentence, then we expire—
with the meaning (Augustine would say "God's meaning")
still in progress of expression, not yet revealed to us. "For a
sentence," writes Augustine,

cannot be completed unless each word of
it, once its syllables have been pronounced,
makes way for the next.

In this world so shot through with unknowns, I wish I
could offer my reader a good, proven way to use question
marks to increase the personal capacity for open questioning—both to make more headway on problems that,

however difficult they look, are ultimately soluble (through open-mindedness) and to induce in us a vitalizing awe, like Augustine's, regarding all the matters that will lie beyond our ken from birth to our last day.

Unfortunately, I don't know of such a use for the question mark. Most sentences that end with that familiar piece of punctuation *don't* encourage inquiry or wonder; they are either informational, as in "Honey, did you get our passports yet?" or strictly rhetorical: "Passports? Am I supposed to be in charge of everything?!"

What I can, however, offer in service to more mindful inquiry and wonder are (a) a passing reminder (these few words are it) of my earlier chapter "Cross-Outs," which overlaps this same terrain, and (b) several thoughts in the following paragraphs about the first-person singular pronoun "I."

In 1976, I had occasion to interview Prof. John Finley, who had been the principal author of Harvard's "Red Book," an ambitious scheme of courses that all Harvard students, regardless of their major, would have to pass to graduate. It was the expression of what Finley and others of his time had thought all educated people ought to know, and it influenced the school experience of undergraduates across America for decades.

When I knocked on his office door in the depths of Harvard's main library, I heard Finley loudly say, "Come in."

I complied, opening the door and crossing his threshold. Then, however, I couldn't find him there. All I saw was his big desk, a wall replete with books, a window that appeared to have no view . . . .

He went right on talking, though, from somewhere.

He invited me to take a seat, in fact. I did—in a chair that faced his desk.

Finley, it turned out, was sitting on the floor behind his desk, turning over cards in a game of solitaire. (Years later, at an event in Finley's memory, one of his friends disclosed that this had been his custom.)

It now seems to me that, by playing solitaire, John Finley was already laying out the theme of our entire conversation: every person's core "solitariness"—the being left alone to make some provisional sense of a world that ultimately proves incomprehensible.

When, at last, Finley rose and sat back down at his desk, he waved his hand around and said,

> Do you see the books that fill this great library? How should we regard them—as the truth? By no means. They are the accounts of human beings attempting to approximate *themselves* to truth.

Graduates of Finley's institution, Harvard, are disproportionately represented in David Halberstam's important book *The Best and the Brightest*, an account of how some well-intentioned, highly educated individuals led a U.S. president into what Halberstam considered one of our most ill-conceived and deadly projects, the Vietnam War. Whether one concurs with Halberstam's view of that conflict, we can all, I think, agree that history—despite the many true achievements that it chronicles—is fairly littered with disasters caused by human beings who claimed to know what they were doing when they did it.

We get it wrong—about a business strategy, troubled members of the family, wars, and life generally. Much of a day, we live deluded.

Is my reader familiar with the word *tome*, meaning a ponderous book whose writer seems to speak with authority? Arguably, tomes on history and foreign policy in the very library where Finley had his office led to the debacle in Southeast Asia. Tomes erroneously "proving" racial differences once perpetuated slavery and set the stage for genocide. Even scientific tomes by the likes of Isaac Newton have, at last, had to yield their place to the Albert Einsteins and Niels Bohrs of a later century, when more salient data about the physical universe was available to mull.

Nor do Bohr and Einstein stand much of a chance to be the final word themselves, for reasons David Hume set forth in the 1700s.

Only after interviewing Finley did I fancifully notice that within the one word *tome* (whose origins go back to Greek, in actuality) two English words can be made out: *to me.*

When I was young, my mother found herself surrounded by my father, my kid brother, and me, three sententious males. Her way to discount our pronouncements was to let us have our say on a subject—nodding all the while, as if in admiration of us, even if she wasn't listening—then just tersely add the words "In . . . Your . . . Opinion." I would not admit it to her, but that jab of hers had real effect on me, tending to sharpen my awareness of the bluster in our voices.

Here's what happens, though, as Henry David Thoreau saw: "We commonly do not remember that it is, after all, always just the first person—that is, 'I'—that is speaking." When it comes home to us that subjective-sounding comments starting with *I* can be readily dismissed or downgraded, many of us strip our thoughts of every sign of their too-fallible source—ourselves— and, instead, speak in the omniscient third person. We come on like self-appointed oracles.

A case in point: We as a society are struggling to answer the question "What encroachment on the rights of privacy is justified now, with acts of terrorism in the news frequently and a growing threat of cyberwarfare?" The all-knowing, disembodied third-person voice in a sentence like "Regrettably, these real dangers can't be taken on except through the elimination of certain rights" will seem more conclusive than the singular, first-person voice in "I can't see how else to deal with terrorism than to do away with certain rights." In reality, of course, these two sentences are equally subjective, but the first attempts to mask its subjectivity: An I-less third person is made to order for the purpose.

And more to the point of mindful wonder in this book, if I get too good at passing my opinions off as unassailable truths, I am likely then to stamp a matter "case closed" even in my own mind as soon as I've weighed in on it publicly, almost willfully disabling my native attribute of curiosity.

Why maintain live consciousness of what unfolds around me if I fancy that, past a certain point, all life is a species of *deja vu*?

I-lessness begets eye-lessness.

Every now and then, someone who's avoided saying "I," in order to appear objective, will reclaim the use of it—not to self-aggrandize, but, on the contrary, to acknowledge mortal limits. In his article "The Most Disgusting of the Pronouns," historian John Clive reviews the work of several great nineteenth century historians who unapologetically employ the first-person pronoun. He then makes of their example a preface to his own grammatical coming-out. By the end, he favorably quotes Martin Duberman's comment,

> . . . when a historian allows more of himself to show—his feelings, fantasies and needs, not merely his skills at information-retrieval, organization, and analysis—he is *less* likely to contaminate the data, simply because there is less pretense that he and it are one.

Clive's long concluding sentence telegraphs its point before it even gets to its main verb:

> For his part, the author of this essay—or, I suppose I should now say I myself . . . .

All the foregoing doesn't mean that *I* can't still be over-used—it can. Probably my reader has, in life, encountered people *too* full of themselves, who wield *I* like a scepter that empowers them to settle each tough question of the day. In the few preceding pages, I have only meant to say that essentially the same risk of self-blinding loftiness exists at the other end of usage also: completely I-less prose. Without an *I* thrown in from time to time (or its equivalent, like " . . . in my opinion" or "How it seems to me is . . ."), I am putting on as problematic a display of self-assuredness as overuse of *I* has long been seen to do.

Insofar as I can tell, one enemy of truth—and of appreciative attending to the world as it presents itself to us in real time—is certainty.

A Hedge Against Preoccupation

The Future Tense and Adverbial Provisos

Each of the last three chapters has set forth grammatical means to greater mindfulness that involve
seeing *through* a barrier—

- seeing *through* an excited state of mind, such as fear
- seeing *through* the legal fiction of possession (even
  while adhering to it for the sake of basic social order)
- seeing *through* false certainty.

The important preposition for the chapter starting here
isn't *through*, it's *around*.

My subject here is *peripheral* vision, the awareness that
enables even someone who is working hard against a dead-
line at her accounting firm to observe—as she stands waiting
on a platform for the next commuter train—that a heavy
flooding of the day before has turned an unremarkable low

hill in a park nearby into an alluring island. (She smiles at the thought of making it a pop-up tourist destination. She gives a moment's thanks to whatever deity produces surprises in the world.)

Also, far more darkly, it was a type of awareness possessed by my late friend George Foldi, a man who had survived the Holocaust by keeping his calm wits about him. Even decades afterward, George could always identify the different means of egress from a local restaurant within two minutes of our entering it for the first time ever.

I take the phrase *peripheral vision* from Alan Watts's discussion of the difference between Western, linear thought and Zen Buddhism. It's the best corrective that I know for a certain, too restrictive narrowing of consciousness that often goes with my commitment to plans I make—that is, tunnel vision.

That ubiquitous auxiliary verb *will*, the signature of most plans, is mainly a good thing. By projecting mental pictures of our world and us forward in time, we keep *moving* forward; it's those very images that provide us with our hopeful, animating sense of direction. I think of Winston Churchill's use of *will* in the dark early days of World War II—in such lines as his "The curse of Hitler will be lifted from our age"— and of New York City's leaders' use of *will* amid the ominous debris—still smoldering—that was all that remained of the World Trade Center on September 11, 2001: "We'll rebuild."

I think, as well, of the many times when, to rally in the face of crises, private individuals like you and me employ that word. "We'll pull through," we say. "We will."

And quite justifiably, of course, we use *will* at countless other, much less dire moments. We call upon it for a million purposes that can't be achieved *except* through our commitment over time: learning Spanish, saving enough money to buy a first home, writing a book . . . . In each case, staying the course seems to require bold appropriation of a grammar that imparts factuality to deeds which may never, strictly speaking, come to pass.

Unfortunately, though, in saying "I will," we jeopardize our own mindfulness.

We may focus so intently on the pictured outcome we hope to achieve that we press into the dim margins of our world the many unforeseeable developments that are going to merit notice, too. In an experiment in which twenty-four radiologists were asked to examine a CT scan of the chest for signs of lung cancer—unaware that a gorilla "the size of a matchbox" appeared on five frames—eighty-three percent *missed* the menacing primate.

Closer to home is the gorilla-like teenage son who barges in on one's peaceful, long-anticipated weekend time intended for completion of a new deck. He blurts out, "You free?", plainly meaning, "I need to talk." If he has been sullenly avoiding one for months, his two-word opening represents a crucial, fleeting opportunity to get brought up to date about his life, and to console or advise him. Nonetheless, the planner/implementer in oneself replies, "Not just now, Joe. Can't you see I'm in the middle of a project?" Through preoccupation, we can even go so far as to mistake our progeny for inconveniences. (Ask a seventy- or eighty-year-old who has been a parent to name the big regrets of his/her life.)

I believe that from the story of a certain spider we might draw a serviceable metaphor for being blindered to the world by plans and preoccupation . . .

I was once told by the gifted late psychologist Kiyo Morimoto that, when still young, he had taken part in early studies of the effects of LSD. According to him, some investigators at the time did a lighthearted side-experiment that never found its way into scholarly journals: They fed acid to spiders. The effect was stunning. Spiders "on trips" constructed webs that were perfectly symmetrical.

That might sound like a positive result, since we associate symmetry with beauty, but in fact spiders would have gone the way of dinosaurs if they behaved so rigidly in life normally. They succeed in making strong, well-anchored webs because they accommodate a web's shape to its surroundings—the pattern of leaves in a rhododendron bush, the irregularities of angle and surface to be discovered high up in the corner of a pantry. The immediate environment nearly always precludes the creation of a shape whose outer lines are equidistant from its center in every direction. What better symbol than a spider high on acid for that willful human being who conducts life with no eye for setting or context?

Ideally, we'd cultivate the vision—peripheral vision—of a good quarterback in football, who uses each successive huddle of his team to announce a next play but then, after the ball has been snapped and the members of both teams fly into action, sizes up what really is developing before him, beyond the play intended. Maybe an opposing tackle has, by unknown means, gone right past the quarterback's defenders and come bearing down on him at full speed now, threatening a "sack" and so a costly setback in yardage. In that case, the quarterback will expeditiously change course. The play that he'd originally called was nothing set in stone; it was a default plan, to be implemented only insofar as circumstance—facts on the ground—permitted.

Similarly, George the Holocaust survivor knew that, necessary as it was to make plans in life (without our plan to have a lunch together monthly, we'd have had to wait years—or forever—to just *happen* to run into each other), one must be ready for anything.

Likewise, a truly mindful hiker knows to set a destination but not let it be her "be-all and end-all." Yes, the vista at the mountain's top is said to be spectacular, but that can't be the sum of what lies waiting for her to experience, going up and down the trail. With enough alertness to the path's edges, she might, for example, notice a tree that has been robbed— stripped in a peculiar pattern—of most of its leaves. Deciding on a momentary pause to investigate the matter, she might next observe a kind of frenzied pileup of moth caterpillars on a branch of that tree close to her, and even note especially a caterpillar scrambling right over one of his stalled siblings to find a less congested, faster route to the disappearing edible foliage that still remains.

She might finally take note, as well, of that tree's immobility, which renders it defenseless in the onslaught and chaos of a moth infestation.

She might then—having registered this all-too-vivid and disturbing proof of Nature's amorality—continue on her way, developing a fuller and more complicated understanding of the natural world than any gorgeous view alone could ever have imparted to her.

The profound problem with *will* statements—"I will finish work on our new deck this weekend," "I'll hike straight up Bald Mountain and get myself a turn at the fabled view from there"—is that, in wedding us to certain plans, they put us at risk of blindered fixation. Like the (quite possibly apocryphal) poor spider on LSD, we fail to respond to what presents itself to us in real time.

How, one may ask, can a speaker avoid the self-blinding effects that often accompany one's use of *will*? Here go three suggestions:

1. **Whenever possible, refrain from saying "will" in the first place.**

    When quite young, I worked in a writing program whose director hung the following words on the wall behind his desk: "Don't Put It in Writing." The incongruity of such a sign's hanging in an office dedicated to the proposition that everyone should write wasn't lost on visitors, but the sign's true meaning was plain enough: "Stay flexible and open. Don't commit yourself until you need to. Try hard not to say, 'I'll do that.' Say, 'That's worth looking into; let's keep it in mind as an option going forward.'"

2. **Return *will* to its original meaning.**

   Etymologically, the verb *will* didn't always smack of fiat—of the implication "It's as good as done"—inducing us, like ambition-sick Lady Macbeths, to "feel . . . the future in the instant." In fact, it was not a future tense verb, it was a present tense verb, *willen*, meaning "will to," "intend to." On occasions when the word *will* is called for, we should probably reclaim that first meaning as our own, at least privately, since it accords much better than the current definition with a human's limits. We should *mean* "intend to."

3. **Do say "will," but work a grammatical escape hatch into your speech or text—a qualifying phrase of the type I call an adverbial proviso:**

   If things go on schedule . . .

   Barring unforeseen developments . . .

   Weather permitting . . .

   All things being equal . . .

   Assuming that no interested party to the plan has a change of heart . . .

   If no better plan occurs to us . . .

   [here, a plug for self-care] If I'm well by then . . .

If I'm not yet feeling overworked by my commitments elsewhere . . .

If the mule don't sick and die . . .

[or, for the religious among us] God willing . . . .

In other words, say, "*Unless other, more important or more time-dependent things come up,* I'll do my taxes this week." A modest grammatical step, I grant. But I credit it, in part, with the fact that, as the years have passed, I see more at the margins of my planned life and remain more open to letting what I find there take precedence at times.

Tolerating Ambiguity

"And"

In 2012, I, like many people, was upset to read that designers of the Martin Luther King, Jr. Memorial in Washington, D.C. had chosen for an inscription words of King that give a grossly distorted impression of him when quoted out of context: "I was a drum major for justice, peace, and righteousness." As the poet Maya Angelou said, that short bit of language made him sound like "an arrogant twit." I was as relieved as most people when a decision came down to remove the quote.

Nonetheless, my understanding of King's character differed from that of his defenders in the press at that time, who seemed to believe that self-aggrandizement was a human tendency that should never be associated with him. Even the *Washington Post* took pains to say that in the sermon from which the quote was lifted, King had "*critiqued* . . . the 'drum major instinct.'"

But he had not. Remarkably, with great self-honesty, King had actually confessed to being *motivated* by the wish to be a larger figure than others. He had said that everybody harbored such a wish. At some length, he had retold the story of disciples James and John, who, in Mark 10:35, "selfishly" ask Jesus to let them sit next to him as his appointed righthand men. King had written,

> Before we condemn them, let us see that we all have the drum major instinct. We all want to be important, to surpass others . . . .

And from there he had gone on, in a loving wit about his audience, to implicate everyone from war-mongering national leaders to the common folk who expend their energy in joining church committees or in shopping to "keep up with the Joneses."

It was not the wish to outdo others that King had attacked—he hadn't seen a way to eradicate that piece of human psychology. ("You just go on living life," he had said, "and you will discover very soon that you like to be praised.") What he had attacked in his sermon was *misdirecting* one's ego, "harnessing it" (his words) to the wrong causes. Only then, he'd said, was it "destructive."

He'd interpreted Jesus's accepting stance toward the two glory-seeking apostles, James and John, to mean,

> Don't give up feeling the need for being first.
> But I want you to be first in love . . . first in moral excellence . . . .

That, as I've read King, was the true context for his resounding lines on how he hoped to be remembered—"If you want to say I was a drum major, say I was a drum major for justice . . ." and so forth.

To King, we human beings weren't egocentric *or* high-minded; we were glaringly self-serving *and* high-minded. What is more, that potentially dyspeptic admixture was, to King, human nature at its best. He bid us all get used to it. He bid us generate as much real good in the world as our paradoxical, inborn psyches permit. There was simply too much need of our committed action in society for us to sit life out on the sidelines, waiting first to be imbued with a purity no one achieves.

King would seem to have been saying what a critic once said in a review of Martin Scorsese's gritty films: "Truth and beauty . . . and depravity . . . must share the same frame"— although King would probably have used a word less damning than *depravity*.

And beyond the moral incongruity that both King and Scorsese came to accept, we have scores of other contradictions in our lives today. I see now that, by the time a reader of this book has turned the last page, he or she will have been treated to a host of aims for life that don't logically accord with each other, despite the fact that they're all attributes of a fully realized person. Take, for example (from early in this book), passivity *and* agency. Or take engaged participation in community *and* more independence from the views of others than communities in general welcome. Those are merely two of the numerous dichotomies I've named and tried to honor here.

Can I, can you, truly hold within our working repertoires such (ostensibly, at least) incompatible pairings and still feel coherent about ourselves—feel, that is, like we have a code to live by?

In my twenties, I read—rather, tried to read—William Empson's *Seven Types of Ambiguity*, in which Empson quotes passages from English literature that can be interpreted in more than one way, classifying each as an example of one of seven esoteric categories he's devised.

I found his book intriguing but exasperating. Also, through it all, I wondered, "Why bother?" Even where, as in most of Empson's sampling, ambiguity reflects a gifted author's intention, not sloppiness, what could be said of it beyond its being clever?

It was not until his last chapter that I heard Empson address that question, and he did so in such a fleeting, offhand manner that for thirty years afterward I imagined that his sentence on the subject appeared in parentheses, although it doesn't:

> The object of life, after all, is not to under-
> stand things, but to maintain one's
> equilibrium and live as well as one can.

As they say, that line alone was worth the price of admission.

Among the chief grammatical enablers of "equilibrium" that Empson names is that all-too-common waif I've mentioned several times already in this chapter, the conjunction *and*. Before reading Empson, I had simply not perceived such high calling in her.

There's no question of it, though. Take a quip of Bertrand Russell's that I stumbled on. Asked to sum up the theology of George Santayana, Russell replied with an *and* paradox that, for all its humor, seems to me to voice the real thinking of millions of people today, who, for their good reasons, maintain lives of faith even while placing great confidence in all the godless findings of science. In Russell's formulation, Santayana's creed was that "there's no God, and the Virgin Mary is his mother."

That's as wonderfully straight-faced a use of "and" as I have seen.

Or take two lines from the preface to one of Jon Kabat-Zinn's most effective meditations for creating mindfulness, the Mountain Meditation. Containing three appearances of *and*, Kabat-Zinn's lines represent a lyrical embrace of contradiction. (Italics have been added.)

> Mountains are held sacred, embodying dread
> *and* harmony, harshness *and* majesty. Rising
> above all else on our planet, they beckon *and*
> overwhelm with their sheer presence.

By calling all such high, paradoxical locations on Earth "sacred," Kabat-Zinn implicitly exempts the highest truth of things from having to adhere to our normal logic.

Other ambiguous *ands* that I have come across include Nicholas Kilmer's "furious, and wild, and peaceful" (about a country scene he was painting) and a colleague's "frightening and sad and exhilarating" (about an impending change in career).

In its way, then, *and* can help us get beyond the either/or mentality that dominates in most speech and writing. *And* can help us keep life's sundry truths all up in the air at once, since we require all of them.

Nick Carraway, F. Scott Fitzgerald's fictional narrator in *The Great Gatsby*, asserts, "Life is much more successfully looked at from a single window," but Fitzgerald himself once said, "The test of a first-rate intelligence is the ability to hold two opposing ideas in the mind at the same time and still retain the ability to function." Whether or not "first-rate intelligence" is the best name for the quality that he refers to (the poet Keats cryptically dubbed it "negative capability"), the need to see and live in poise among competing valid claims on our attention is hard to deny.

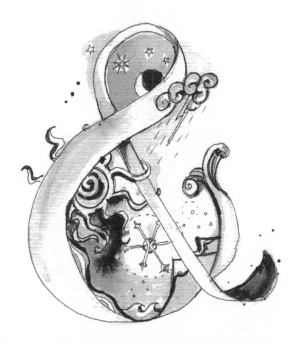

GRAMMAR FOR
THE END

Our Dying

Order . . . Then Gibberish and Silence

What does it mean to be a self-conscious animal? The idea is ludicrous, if it is not monstrous. It means to know that one is food for worms.
— ERNEST BECKER, *THE DENIAL OF DEATH*

Humankind cannot bear very much reality.
— T. S. ELIOT, *FOUR QUARTETS*

I t should not surprise us that death has come up numerous times in these pages. It's a penumbral shadow hanging over all we do, beginning on the fateful day in childhood when we get wind of it. As Ernest Becker and others in the realm of psychology have shown, sex may be a biggish motivator for us, but it doesn't merit the commanding place in consciousness that Freud accords it. There's a more compelling case for giving center stage to our almost lifelong knowledge of a human's finitude: the fact that, despite our extraordinary consciousness and other gifts, we don't last forever.

It's a reality that we are simply not built for accepting. For that reason, we adopt comforting beliefs about an afterlife (one or more of these could even prove true—what do I know?); attach ourselves to institutions, groups, and causes likely to outlast us; undertake impressive, death-defying feats on battlefields and elsewhere that might satisfy our hope that we're a match for death . . . or assure us of a lasting spot in others' memories; have children who will carry DNA of ours into the future; behave so well that God would have to make a special case of us; fill our days with so much frantic stir and fussing that we have no time for thoughts of personal extinction; get high daily . . . .

Also, as with most needs, we address our need to deal with death partly through grammar, which, in fact, has made some useful contributions to the cause. These support our happiness without being *overly* delusional—so divorced from normal understandings of the world as to undermine our functioning.

First of all, grammar quietly allays the fear of death by making us feel "orderly."

I have read that grammarian Dominique Bouhours's last words were:

> I am about to—or I am going to—die. Either
> expression is used.

What fabulous humor. Also, though, what resilient, down-to-the-wire defiance of that jumbled fate we pass into without consciousness, on breathing our last.

Physiologically speaking, we are exquisitely *well-organized* beings, and we rightly fear that our survival depends on staying "in good order." (Tellingly, we call our ailments *dis*orders.) As an ever-present model of order, grammar—whenever we have shown that we can handle it correctly—makes us feel intact and healthy.

I once wrote a play in which a member of the clergy keeps up his and others' faith by diagramming sentences.

The sad, dissolving grammar that sets in if someone's mind becomes disorganized prior to death is among the first signs of that person's return to the nonverbal welter that once birthed us all and awaits us. I call it (with affection please) the grammar of gibberish, and my latest glimpse of it could not have been more poignant.

A woman for whom words had always mattered—a dear friend of mine who'd partnered with me to found Harvard's Writing Center in 1976, and subsequently authored the most popular book on how to write a Ph.D. dissertation—came with her husband to my home for dinner. I had heard she had dementia, but I hadn't known how it expressed itself.

She launched a thousand comments and left every one adrift, without clearly joining any subject to its predicate: "It's not one, two . . . ," "Never bites" (about her dog, I think), "You could person . . . you know, go achoo." At one point, she seemed to be attempting to get back the simple word "family," saying, "My, uhhh . . . my . . . four people . . . ."

Through it all, I sensed that she still recognized me and felt warmly toward me. Otherwise, I'd have found the evening devastating.

What are words but just our voiced distinctions—labels used to isolate and differentiate one thing from another in the overwhelming field of vision confronting us in infancy? We term the *inert, brownish* object on four legs a chair and the *moving, furry* object on four legs a golden retriever. In the end, of course—not just for my colleague with dementia, but for each of us—all distinctions vanish, unless there is an afterlife.

Poet George Ellenbogen found himself aboard a train headed for Yugoslavia. Sharing his compartment was a woman missing one of her arms, the awful price exacted by a bomb some unknown person had delivered to her home during ethnic hostilities. But when Ellenbogen got around at last to writing a poem about the woman, "Night Train to Zagreb," he had forgotten which side of the conflict her enemy belonged to.

> It was a Serb. Or was it a Croat?
> who came out of a night like this
> with candlesticks . . .

It was just as well the poet had forgotten. Deftly, he parlays his private loss of memory into a reverie of sorts about distinction-making generally. The snow the poet sees hitting his window on the train

> . . . separates in alphabet,
> the vowels clinging to glass,
> consonants slipping into drifts.

We and all the vitally important distinctions that we make with words won't endure, but by maintaining order in our bodies and our words we keep the specter of demise at bay.

But enough of that. The appearance of abiding order isn't grammar's only means of countering the death-effect in life.

Secondly—at least for those of us who put some words in writing—language is a tangible extension of ourselves that has a longer shelf-life than we ourselves do. We imagine it, and therefore us, continuing to live well beyond some engraved end-date on display in a cemetery. Anne Sexton called her cache of poems her "immortality box."

Finally, with grammar's help, we engage in that harmless form of magical thinking whereby we are sure to go on living through the words of *others*, when such words describe or celebrate us in the future. In his Sonnet 18, Shakespeare lavishes praise on a certain young man, claiming that his beauty outdoes that of a summer's day. Then, with remarkable boldness, he tells him not to fear that his looks will undergo the usual last phase of death and decay. How so? Shakespeare waves the sheet of words he has produced—the very sonnet we've been reading—and proclaims,

So long lives this, and this gives life to thee.

My father was a person not as given to magical thoughts about death—or to belief in an afterlife—as most of us are.

On November 26, 1988, I picked up a ringing phone at my home. It was my father, curtly saying, "Larry, is that you?"

"Dad?" I asked him, though I knew for certain who it was, then said, "Yes, me."

"I'm calling you about Mom."

There was silence . . . which I dared not break, although it went too long.

"Yeah," my father said at last, as if I had already put a second question to him.

I hadn't even known my mother was ill, and now, incredibly, I could tell she must be gone from all the world.

My father's shocking wordlessness might be explained different ways, but by the time I wrote a play about grammar years later (the one in which a minister diagrams sentences), I'd concluded that his silence was perfectly in line with his unusually hard-bitten type of realism. He was mute because the words "your mother" could no longer mean what they had meant before. As I have a high school English teacher in my play say, in his suicide note to a former student,

> Fierson, don't let me or my end haunt you.
> Don't imagine I continue to exist past
> death. Immortality, insofar as I can tell, is,
> ironically, a myth brought into being by
> grammar. If I tell you, "Mr. Grassley is dead,"
> unfortunately I must preserve Mr. Grassley
> intact—spelled exactly as he was when
> living—or my sentence has no subject, and
> that summons me to life in your mind's eye
> just as it always did . . . but the truth is, there
> is no such thing as Mr. Grassley any longer.

It was a relief to me that, when my father died, he died at peace. He brought that off partly by acceding, at long last, to the sort of grammatical confusion which spares most of us some of the terror attached to life's end. He used linguistic ambiguity to complicate—or soften—the *difference* between life and death. Not long before he passed, he informed me that he liked the saying "Death is *part* of life."

Coda

The Comedienne of Grammar

Grammar, then, can serve a multitude of needs, when it's handled with intention.

Perhaps the world's best-known grammatical joke is the one with which vaudevillians George Burns and Gracie Allen closed every episode of their television show in the 1950s. George would say,

> Say "Good night," Gracie.

and the scatterbrained Gracie, misunderstanding where the quotation marks fell in George's request, would always sweetly respond,

> Good night, Gracie.

It therefore seems appropriate that Gracie's last act of love toward George, who was her real-life husband of thirty-eight years, should also involve some grammatical wit. Rumor has it that she left a note for him to find after she died, a plea to him to go on living: "Never place a period where God has put a comma."

My own wife, when dying, did much the same for me, in language I'll be keeping to myself.

In my view, no one still up to the task of uttering a brand-new sentence is not also capable of growing more whole daily. May that livening experience—and true gladness for the chance of it, as well—be my reader's fate.

— LW

Sources and Endnotes

Page v. *"To tell how near . . . ."* Nachman of Bratzlav, *Garden of the Souls: Rebbe Nachman on Suffering,* ed. Avraham Greenbaum (Monsey, NY: Breslov Research Institute, 1990). Quotation from p. 40.

INTRODUCTION

Page 1. *"The limits of my . . . ."* Ludwig Wittgenstein, *Tractatus Logico-Philosophicus,* trans. C. K. Ogden (New York: Cosimo Classics, 2007). Quotation from p. 88.

Page 3. *Then, I stumbled on . . . .* Benjamin Whorf, *Language, Thought, and Reality,* ed. John B. Carroll (Cambridge, MA: MIT Press, 1956). See pp. 221, 269.

Page 4. *I soon learned . . . .*

For a good introduction to the controversy that surrounds Whorf, see John H. McWhorter's *The Language Hoax* (New York: Oxford University Press, 2014).

GRAMMAR TO TAKE LIFE IN HAND

Page 8. *"Even God dare not . . . ."* "Gandhiji in Lancashire," *Young India: A Weekly Journal*, 13.42 (October 15, 1931). Quotation from p. 310.

Page 8. *Like the American psychologist Abraham Maslow . . . .* A. H. Maslow, "A Theory of Human Motivation," *Psychological Review*, 50 (1943): pp. 370-396.

Page 8. *To my understanding . . . .*

Philosophically, the existence of free will may be hard to prove, but "agency"—the enlivening *perception* that we're free and capable of acts that will make a difference—is a hardwired need. Without it, we human beings languish. We lead "lives of quiet desperation," as Thoreau put it, or resort to behaviors meant to bring down others with us. At the far end of decline, such hopelessness leaves a person literally bedridden, as researcher Ellen Langer has shown.

GETTING NOTICED

Page 10. *"If I am not . . . ."* Rabbi Hillel, *Pirkei Avot 1:14* (a tractate of the Mishna composed of ethical maxims).

Page 11. *"a lot less attractive."* Lewis Thomas, *The Medusa and the Snail: More Notes of a Biology Watcher* (New York: Viking Press, 1979). Quotation from p. 104.

Page 12. *"felt it was worse . . . ."* William Strunk, Jr. and E. B. White, *The Elements of Style*, 2nd ed. (New York: Macmillan, 1972). Quotations from pp. 9, 2, and xii.

Tapping Inborn Energy

Page 16. *"the striving for perfection."* Heinz Ludwig Ansbacher and Rowena R. Ansbacher, *Individual Psychology of Alfred Adler* (New York: HarperCollins, 1956). Quotation from p. 104.

Page 22. *"serves as a cop-out . . . ."* Albert Ellis and Robert Harper, *A New Guide to Rational Living* (Englewood Cliffs, NJ: Prentice Hall, 1975). Quotation from p. xiv.

The Wherewithal

Page 24. *It demands adding . . . .*

One grammatical alternative to prepositional phrases worth mentioning is descriptive phrases that begin with *ing* verbs:

> *Holding* the pole vault in both hands—and *fixing* her gaze on her goal as she picked up speed—Madison cleared the crossbar.

> *Employing* many short, simple sentences, the reporter kept his prose taut.

Doing What Works

Page 29. *"White men and women . . . ."* John Dawkins, "Teaching Punctuation as a Rhetorical Tool." *College*

Composition and Communication, 46.4 (December 1995): pp. 533–48. Alice Walker quoted on p. 539.

Page 29. "*In saying 'The tumult . . . .'*" Margaret Bryant and Janet Rankin Aiken, *Psychology of English* (New York: Columbia University Press, 1940). Quotation from p. 70.

PRESSED FOR TIME

Page 33. "*Boy, this is a . . . .*" Teri Kwal Gamble and Michael W. Gamble, *The Communication Playbook* (Thousand Oaks, CA: SAGE Publications, 2018). Quotation from p. 98.

"NO EFFORT WITHOUT ERROR"

Page 37. "*Ernest Hemingway: I rewrote . . . .*" Interviewer George Plimpton, "Ernest Hemingway, The Art of Fiction, No. 21." *The Paris Review*, 18 (Spring 1958).

Page 37. "*Getting it wrong is . . . .*" Nabeel Hamdi, *Small Change* (London: Taylor & Francis, 2013). Charles Handy quoted on p. 140.

Page 38. "*There seems to be . . . .*" *Charles Darwin*, ed. Philip Strong Humphrey (New York: Scribner, 1956). Quotation from p. 28.

Page 38. *On the contrary.*

Having produced a draft and seen no reason to make cross-outs in it often indicates a writer who has yet to live at her mind's frontier, breaking new ground. The heuristic payoffs of a cross-out habit are enormous.

The influential behavioral psychologist B. F. Skinner once told me that he made such messes with revision in his writing that, to leave space for them all, he customarily used sheets of paper that measured 22 by 34 inches, a surface area eight times that of a normal sheet of paper. More importantly, he referred back to those "messes" when I asked him how it was that he could wake at 5:00 a.m. every day, go straight to his writing desk, and remain there for several hours. I had expected his answer to be something like "Gum drops," since his fame rested on his showing the power of external rewards (positive reinforcement) to induce animals—including human beings—to perform whatever acts the person who's dispensing rewards wishes them to. (By this means, he had taught pigeons to play ping-pong.) But Skinner's response to my question had nothing to do with externals. What drove him back to his desk every morning was, he said, the revelation that, by means of messy drafting, he could always make real progress in his thinking.

Page 40–41. "*Novelists . . . have, on the . . . .*" Kurt Vonnegut, *Palm Sunday* (New York: Dial Press, 2011). Quotation from p. 116.

Page 41. "*It is not the critic . . . .*" Theodore Roosevelt, "Citizenship in a Republic" (speech), Paris, France. 1910.

Grammar for Creative Passivity

Page 44. "*The right shot . . . .*" Eugen Herrigel, *Zen in the Art of Archery* (New York: Vintage Books, 1989). Quotation from pp. 50–51.

GETTING OUT OF ONE'S OWN WAY

Page 47. "*Suppose that you . . . kill . . . .*" William James, *Talks to Teachers on Psychology: And to Students on Some of Life's Ideals* (New York: Henry Holt, 1925). Quotation from p. 152.

Page 48. "*Use the active voice . . . .*" William Strunk, Jr. and E. B. White, *The Elements of Style*, 2nd ed. (New York: Macmillan, 1972). Quotation from p. 13.

Page 48. "*Politics and the English Language.*" A George Orwell essay in *Horizon*, 13.76 (April 1946): pp. 252–265.

Page 49. "*Mr. Bruce suffers from . . . .*" ed. Lisa Grunwald and Stephen J. Adler, *Letters of the Century* (New York: Dial Press, 2008). Quotation from p. 422.

Page 49. *By contrast to the stance . . . .* Otto Jespersen, *The Philosophy of Grammar* (New York: W. W. Norton, 1924). See pp. 167–168.

Page 50. *Think of all the factors.*

Philosopher Michael Sandel makes the point ingeniously (and more broadly than I) in the form of a fictitious letter of college admission:

Dear *[successful applicant]*,

We are pleased to inform you that your application for admission has been accepted. It turns out that you happen to have the traits that society needs at the moment, so we propose to exploit your assets for society's advantage by admitting you to the study of [name of subject].

You are congratulated, not in the sense that you deserve credit for having [these qualities]—you do not—but only in the sense that the winner of the lottery is to be congratulated. You are lucky to have come along with the right traits at the right moment . . . .

You, or more likely your parents, may be tempted to . . . take this admission to reflect favorably, if not on your native endowments, then at least on the conscientious effort you have made to cultivate your abilities. But the notion that you deserve even the superior character necessary to your effort is equally problematic, for your character depends on fortunate circumstances of various kinds for which you can claim no credit. The notion of dessert does not apply here.

We look forward nonetheless to seeing you in the fall.

Sincerely yours . . .

— SOURCE: *JUSTICE: WHAT'S THE RIGHT THING TO DO?*, BY MICHAEL J. SANDEL

Page 54. *Now, as we talk or poke away.*

For scores of examples beyond my own here, see Daniel Kahneman's compelling *Thinking, Fast and Slow* (New York: Farrar, Straus and Giroux, 2011).

Page 54. "*the tacit dimension.*" Michael Polanyi, *The Tacit Dimension* (Chicago: University of Chicago Press, 2009).

ACTIVE-PASSIVE HYBRID NO. 1

Page 57. "*Teach us to care . . . .*" T. S. Eliot, *The Complete Poems and Plays* (New York: Harcourt, Brace and World, 1971). Quotation from p. 67.

Page 58. "*naïve notion of an . . . .*" Benjamin Whorf, *Language, Thought, and Reality*, ed. John B. Carroll (Cambridge, MA: The MIT Press, 2012). Quotation from p. 312.

ACTIVE-PASSIVE HYBRID NO. 2

Page 61. "*Pain—has an Element . . . .*" Emily Dickinson, *The Complete Poems*, ed. Thomas H. Johnson (Boston: Little, Brown and Co., 1960). Quotation from p. 323.

Page 61. "*When a thought takes . . . .*" Emily Dickinson, *Selected Poems*, ed. Conrad Aiken (New York: Modern Library, 1948). Quotation by Thomas Wentworth Higginson from p. viii.

Page 62. "*Pain has an Element . . . .*" Emily Dickinson, *Poems*, ed. Mabel Loomis Todd and T. W. Higginson (Boston: Little, Brown and Co., 1910). Quotation from p. 33.

Page 62. *"habit of handwriting."* R. W. Franklin, *The Editing of Emily Dickinson: A Reconsideration* (Madison, WI: University of Wisconsin Press, 1967). Quotation from p. 120.

Page 64. *"Not knowing when the . . . ."* Emily Dickinson, *The Selected Poems of Emily Dickinson* (Hertfordshire, England: Wordsworth Editions, 1994). Quotation from p. 129.

Grammar for Belonging

Page 66. *"If I am not . . . ."* Rabbi Hillel, *Pirkei Avot 1:14* (a tractate of the Mishna composed of ethical maxims).

Wondrous Touch

Page 69. *"warm, imaginative touch."* John Trimble, *Writing with Style: Conversations on the Art of Writing* (Englewood Cliffs, NJ: Prentice Hall, 1975). Quotation from p. 19.

Page 70. *"Someone walks in . . . ."* Walker Gibson, *The "Speaking Voice" and the Teaching of Composition* (New York: College Entrance Examination Board, 1965). Quotation from p. 6.

The Russian linguist Lev Vygotsky makes much the same point by citing a long passage in Dostoevsky's *The Diary of a Writer*, in which six young workmen manage to conduct a whole conversation using only one potent swear word but investing it with new meaning on each utterance through vocal inflection and gesture.

Page 71–72. "*Gentlemen: Here I am . . . .*" Lisa Grunwald and Stephen J. Adler, eds., *Letters of the Century* (New York: Dial Press, 1999). Quotation from p. 571.

Page 72. "*Punctuation—just one of . . . .*" John Dawkins, "Teaching Punctuation as a Rhetorical Tool," *College Composition and Communication*, 46.4 (December 1995): pp. 533–48. Quotation from p. 533.

Page 73. "*Hideously infrared divergent.*" Sidney Coleman and Erick Weinberg, "Radiative Corrections as the Origin of Spontaneous Symmetry Breaking," *Physical Review D*, 7.6 (March 1973): pp. 1888–1910.

CLEAR MESSAGING

Page 75. "*One shouldn't aim . . . .*" Quintilian, *The Orator's Education*, book 8.2.

Page 80. *First, the interested reader . . . .*

The main point of Lynne Truss's popular *Eats, Shoots and Leaves* is very much in keeping with mine in this chapter. Her book's title is, in fact, a fine example of that point—just remove the comma after *Eats* and observe how the meaning of her title changes.

BONDING

Page 83. "*This is Just . . . .*" William Carlos Williams, *Selected Poems* (New York: New Directions, 1968). Quotation from p. 55.

Page 84. *"[The person] who pays . . . ."* E. E. Cummings, *Collected Poems* (San Diego, CA: Harcourt, Brace, 1938). Quotation from p. 180.

Page 84. *We can make . . . use of silence . . . .*

Another good linguistic means of bonding—one I haven't referenced in this chapter, since it goes beyond grammar—is to shift diction to a level one's reader/listener is comfortable at. It's saying "clothes" instead of "attire" and "Yeah, thanks, I get it" instead of "Yes, I fully comprehend that." The finest case I know is a revision of a speech of Franklin Delano Roosevelt's in the 1930s. FDR's writer handed him a line that, in tone, sounded like the stilted term papers students write at prestigious universities:

> We are endeavoring to construct a more inclusive society.

FDR was having none of it. He replaced the line with

> We're going to make a country in which no one is left out.

—a sentence whose plain words ensured no *listener* to it got "left out."

A DEFENSE OF CORRECTNESS

Page 87. "*A language is a . . . .*" Max Weinreich, "Der YIVO un di problemen fun undzer tsayt," *YIVO Bletter* 25.1 (January–February 1945): pp. 3–18. Quotation from p. 13.

EMPATHIZING

Page 91–92. "*10. From Alexander the grammarian . . . .*" Marcus Aurelius, *Meditations* (London: Watkins Media, 2014). Quotation from p. 3.

Page 93. "*Giving reason.*" Eleanor Duckworth, *The Having of Wonderful Ideas and Other Essays on Teaching and Learning* (New York: Teachers College Press, 1996).

Page 94. "*If a person* knew . . . .*" Jun Lim, *Socrates: The Public Conscience of Golden Age Athens* (New York: Rosen Publishing, 2005). Socrates quoted on p. 62.

Of course, in this life, we have both "knowing" (superficial understanding) and real *knowing*. Here, Socrates meant something more than the ability to mouth a truth one doesn't fully grasp and accept yet.

GENEROSITY

Page 97. "*Isn't ready . . . .*" John Trimble, *Writing with Style: Conversations on the Art of Writing* (Englewood Cliffs, NJ: Prentice Hall, 1975). Quotation from p. 101.

Page 97. *"It is as though . . . ."* Trudy Govier, *A Practical Study of Argument* (Boston: Cengage Learning, 2013). Quotation by Albert Einstein from p. 319.

Page 98. *"I could not imagine . . . ."* Annie Dillard, *The Writing Life* (New York: Harper and Row, 1990). Quotations from pp. 99, 100, and 105.

Page 98. *"It is almost always . . . ."* Lewis Thomas, *The Medusa and the Snail: More Notes of a Biology Watcher* (New York: Viking Press, 1979). Quotation from p. 104.

Page 99–100. *"modify the statement . . . ."* Francis Christensen, *Notes toward a New Rhetoric: Six Essays for Teachers* (New York: Harper and Row, 1978). Quotations from pp. 5 and 12.

To Compromise but Not Be "Compromised"

Page 102. *"There is nothing stable . . . ."* ed. Grant F. Scott, *Selected Letters of John Keats* (Cambridge, MA: Harvard University Press, 2002). Quotation from p. 70.

Page 103. *"Acute, tuned up . . . ."* John Barth, *The End of the Road* (New York: Bantam Books, 1969). Quotation from p. 134.

Page 106–107. *"When feasible, use plural . . . ."* Maxine C. Hairston, *Successful Writing* (New York: W. W. Norton, 1981). Quotations from pp. 124–26.

Page 107. *"Prefer geniality to . . . ."* Henry Watson Fowler and Francis George Fowler, *The King's English* (Oxford, England: Clarendon Press, 1930). Quotation from p. 70.

Page 108. *"Must modify itself if . . . ."* Eric Partridge, *Usage and Abusage* (New York: Norton and Company, 1997). Quotation from p. 134.

GRAMMAR FOR FREEDOM

Page 110. *"I have known . . . ."* T. S. Eliot, "The Love Song of J. Alfred Prufrock," *The Complete Poems and Plays* (New York: Harcourt, Brace and World, 1971). Quotation from p. 5.

DISTINGUISHING HOW YOU'RE PERCEIVED FROM WHO YOU ARE

Page 114. *"You stop being a pest now . . . ."* Thomas Gordon, *P.E.T.—Parent Effectiveness Training: The Tested New Way to Raise Responsible Children* (New York: New American Library, 1975). Quotation from p. 121.

A caveat is in order here, however. In the wrong tone of voice, I-statements can prove fully as damning as accusatory you-statements. One generally good book on child-rearing surprisingly offers the following I-tirade as a model I-statement: "When I see all of you rush away from dinner to watch TV, and leave me with the dirty dishes and greasy pans, I feel murderous! I feel like taking every dish and breaking it on the TV set!"

Other False Equations

Page 116. "*The little word . . . .*" George Santayana, *Scepticism and Animal Faith: Introduction to a System of Philosophy* (New York: Dover Publications, 1955). Quotation from p. 71.

Page 117. "*May be a very . . . .*" Alfred Korzybski, *Science and Sanity: An Introduction to Non-Aristotelian Systems and General Semantics* (Fort Worth, TX: Institute of General Semantics, 1958). Quotation from p. 758.

Page 117. "*The mind is ever-changing . . . .*" Peter Harvey, *An Introduction to Buddhism: Teachings, History and Practices* (New York: Cambridge University Press, 2003). Quotation from p. 280.

Page 118. David Bourland, Jr. *To Be or Not to Be: E-Prime as a Tool for Critical Thinking* (Institute of General Semantics, http://www.esgs.org/uk/art/epr1.htm).

The Linguistic Limits to Freedom

Page 123. *All I can propose . . . .*

The only other grammatical ploy that comes to mind for distancing one's current, whole, evolving self from past or partial selves is recourse to the third person. It's the path Shakespeare's Hamlet takes when he tells Laertes, whose father Hamlet has unintentionally killed in a frenzy and whose sister he's driven to suicide, "Hamlet does it not, Hamlet denies it. Who does it, then? His madness." Unfortunately, though, this third-person solution is hazardous. It corresponds roughly to what became known in politics as "compartmentalization" during the 1990s. Taken too far, it can lead to wrong conduct with impunity, a life of aliases.

Page 123. "*Then the Lord God . . . .*" Genesis 3:19.

HAVING ONE'S OWN WAY OF SEEING

Page 125. "*Whoever fills his life . . . .*" Abraham Isaac Kook, *Olat Raiyeh* (commentary on the Jewish prayer book).

Page 127. "*[This type of] imitation . . . .*" Jean Piaget, *The Language and Thought of the Child* (London: Routledge, 2002). Quotation from p. 12.

Page 127. *By and by, of course . . . .*

I have heard it said by some postmodernists that we are *always* quoting—that there's no real "me" under the compulsive imitator, one's persona. As my reader probably can tell, I don't feel prepared to say that yet.

Page 127. "*Knowing what you really . . . .*" Ernest Hemingway, *Death in the Afternoon* (New York: Simon and Schuster, 2002). Quotation from p. 11.

Page 129. "*The scent of these . . . .*" Jimmie Killingsworth, *Whitman's Poetry of the Body* (Chapel Hill, NC: University of North Carolina Press, 1991). Quotation from p. 30.

Page 129. *"Can take a bath . . . ."* Delmore Schwartz, "Does Existentialism Still Exist?", *Partisan Review* 15 (December 1948): pp. 1361–1363.

FRIENDS IN THE GRAVEYARD

Page 132. *Of all my comforters . . . .* Michel de Montaigne, *The Autobiography of Michel de Montaigne*, ed. Marvin Lowenthal (Boston and New York: Houghton Mifflin, 1935). See p. 283. Quotations from pp. 80 and 142.

Page 133. *"No activity can become . . . ."* Hannah Arendt, *The Portable Hannah Arendt*, ed. Peter R. Baehr (New York: Penguin Classics, 2003). Quotation from p. 199.

Page 133–134. *"Like ghosts from an . . . ."* Percy Bysshe Shelley, *The Poetical Works of Percy Bysshe Shelley*, ed. Mary Wollstonecraft Shelley (London: E. Moxon, 1839). Quotation from p. 249.

Page 134. *Anna in the Tropics*, play by Nilo Cruz (New York: Theatre Communications Group, 2003).

Page 134. *"Up to then, I . . . ."* Malcolm X and Alex Haley, *The Autobiography of Malcolm X* (New York: Ballantine Books, 1992). Quotation from p. 173.

Page 134. *"Later . . . in a more . . . ."* C. P. Cavafy, "Hidden Things," *My Business is Circumference: Poets on Influence and Mastery* (Philadelphia: Paul Dry Books, 2001). Quotation from p. 79.

Page 134. "*Read there, in plain view . . . .*" Marcus Aurelius, *Meditations* (Chicago: Henry Regency Co., 1956). See p. xiii.

FULCRUM

Page 139. "*We fight, but the . . . .*" Angela Hunt, *Concerning War, Volume 1: A Collection of Recollections with Room for Rumination* (Gilbert, MN: Range PrintWorks: 2017). Quotation from p. 142.

Page 140. "*a Heav'n of Hell . . . .*" John Milton, *Paradise Lost*, ed. Merritt Y. Hughes (Indianapolis: Bobbs-Merrill, 1962). Quotation from p. 13.

Page 141. "*But if a man . . . .*" *Treatises and Sermons of Meister Eckhart*, ed. James Midgley Clark and John Vass Skinner (New York: Harper, 1958).

Page 142–143. "*When you start looking . . . .*" Nachman of Bratzlav, *Likutey Moharan*, ed. Ozer Bergman and Moshe Mykoff (Jerusalem: Breslov Research Institute, 1995).

Page 144. *In the end, yes . . . .*

For a word so useful in achieving self-renewal—by which I mean the sense of being altogether "okay" with the world, ready to participate in it again freely, with no shame—*but* has an unfortunate, curt sound to it. It should sport at least one long, inviting open vowel. It shouldn't smack so much of utilitarian glumness. I prefer its more vibrant Spanish equivalent, *pero*.

Grammar, Thing of Beauty

Page 145. *"Don't hide your light . . . ."* Luke 8:16–18.

Page 145. *"Grammar is a piano . . . ."* Joan Didion, "Why I Write," in *Joan Didion: Essays and Conversations,* ed. Ellen G. Friedman (Princeton, NJ: Ontario Review Press, 1984). Quotation from p. 7.

Page 146. *I might put off naming . . . .*

I was torn here between using my sentence about ants and using a whole passage of mine about glitter. In the latter, unused passage—a short text about the unexpected places in a house where old glitter will turn up, inserted below—the word itself, "glitter," puts in its appearance at a different, unexpected place in each sentence: first, in subject position ("My loose glitter gets . . ."); then, at the remote far end of a sentence's main verb (". . . quietly there dwells more glitter"); and finally as the object of the preposition in an embedded phrase (". . . of glitter . . ."). That is, the passage is designed to give *readers* the experience of encountering glitter in locations that can't be predicted.

> The problem with my using glitter is that, after I have thought I cleaned it up, I keep finding remnants of the stuff everywhere. My loose glitter gets into the far, dark corners of my floor. In the cuffs of my worn jeans, quietly there dwells more glitter. If I stick a hand into my pocket—or the spaces

between cushions on my sofa—I'll come up with particles of glitter for unending years into the future.

Page 146–147. "*Not too long ago . . . .*" Barbara Ehrenreich, *The Worst Years of Our Lives* (New York: Pantheon Books, 1990). Quotation from p. 22.

Page 147. "*It does not seem . . . .*" Malcolm Gladwell, "Annals of Commerce: The Terrazzo Jungle," *The New Yorker* (March 15, 2004): pp. 120–27. Quotation from pp. 121–22.

Page 148–149. "*Miguel Maldonado is nineteen . . . .*" Richard Currey, *Crossing Over: The Vietnam Stories* (Livingston, MT: Clark City Press, 1993). Quotation from pp. 25–26.

Page 149. "*To take [one's] agony . . . .*" Joe McGinniss, *Heroes* (New York: Viking Press, 1976). Quotation from p. 121.

Page 149. "*We pull each . . . .*" James Frey, *A Million Little Pieces* (New York: Anchor Books, 2005). Quotation from pp. 307–308.

Page 150. "*The show was over . . . .*" Annie Dillard, *The Writing Life* (New York: Harper and Row, 1990). Quotations from pp. 97–98.

The unrevised original reads,

The show was over. It was late.

Just as I turned from the runway, something caught my eye and made me laugh.

It was a swallow, having its own air show, apparently inspired by Rahm. The swallow climbed high over the runway, held its wings oddly, tipped them, and rolled down the air in loops.

Grammar for Mindfulness

Page 154. *"Hear, O Israel . . . ."* Deuteronomy 6:4.

Avoiding Hype and Fearfulness

Page 156. *"Human noises vexed the . . . ."* Thorkild Jacobsen, *The Harps that Once . . . : Sumerian Poetry in Translation* (New Haven, CT: Yale University Press, 1987). Quotation from p. 147.

Page 158. *"Look! they say . . . ."* Lewis Thomas, *The Medusa and the Snail: More Notes of a Biology Watcher* (New York: Viking Press, 1979). Quotation from pp. 104–105.

Taking Ownership with a Grain of Salt

This chapter had its inception in a silent joke of Mo McGrath, who was a student at Bentley University twenty years ago or so. She once volunteered to organize my handouts on punctuation, which were in disarray. Carefully, she set up a folder labeled "Tense Agreement," another labeled "Proper Citation Form," and so on. By the time she neared her project's end, however, Mo's creative side was clamoring for full expression. She mischievously took a folder of my notes on capitalization and labeled it "Capitalism." Ever since, I have been wondering if grammar could have anything to do with our economy.

Page 162. *"It is easier for . . . ."* Matthew 19:24.

Page 164. *As Adam Smith . . . .* See Genesis Rabbah 9:7.

Page 165. *"Carried off . . . ."* Henry David Thoreau, *Walden* (London: Pan Macmillan, 2010). Quotation from p. 89.

Page 165–166. *"I have met with . . . ."* Henry David Thoreau, *Walking* (Thomaston, ME: Tilbury House Publishers, 2017).

Page 166. *"The secret of successful sauntering."*

For a contrast to Thoreau's view here, consider, for instance, this old Anti-Loitering Ordinance of Athens, Georgia: "All able-bodied persons *wandering, strolling, ambling about* shall be deemed loiterers and apprehended."

Page 166. *"my house . . . ."*

I was struck the other day to read an essay by the actor Steve Martin about Edward Hopper's painting "Captain Upton's House." Legally speaking, Martin *owns* the painting, but in his piece he never says so or uses a possessive pronoun. Here's an excerpt:

> Turning on the living room lights, I see Hopper's "Captain Upton's House." I look over at my wife, Anne, and say in wonder, "How did this happen?" Living with a paint-ing for years brings a different experience

than seeing it reproduced or occasionally
visiting it in a museum . . . .

— Source: *Edward Hopper's Maine*,
edited by Kevin Salatino

Without knowing Martin, I can't help but wonder if his
spirit is somewhat akin to Thoreau's freeing sense of
dispossession.

Uncertainty

Page 168. *"Are you still capable . . ."* Lao Tze, *Tao Te Ching*
(New York: Penguin Random House, 1963). Quotation
from p. 66.

Page 169. *"Uncertainty is a threat . . . ."* Donald Schön, *The
Reflective Practitioner: How Professionals Think in Action*
(New York: Basic Books, 1983). Quotation from p. 69.

Page 170. *As students of cognition . . . .* Abigail Lipson,
"Learning: A Momentary Stay Against Confusion,"
Teaching and Learning: Journal of Natural Inquiry, 6.3
(1990): pp. 2–11.

Page 171. *"For a sentence . . . ."* Saint Augustine, *The Confessions;
The City of God; On Christian Doctrine* (Chicago:
Encyclopædia Britannica, Incorporated, 1990). Quotation
from p. 29.

Page 172. *In 1976 . . . .*

What follows is my memory of John Finley's words. I
have not been able to locate a transcript of the interview

that I conducted with him as part of a pedagogical experiment of Harvard's writing program.

Page 173. *It now seems to me . . . .*

Partly because Finley's field was Classics, I couldn't help but think of Plato's "allegory of the cave" as I sat there in his sunless office, listening to him meditate on the limits of our understanding.

Page 174. *"For reasons David Hume set forth . . . ."* David Hume, *An Enquiry Concerning Human Understanding* (Chelmsford, MA: Courier Corporation, 2004). See Sections IV-VII.

Page 175. *"We commonly do not . . . ."* Henry David Thoreau, *Walden* (London: Pan Macmillan, 2010). Quotation from p. 7. (I have interpolated the words "that is, 'I.'")

Someone who has bothered to count the appearances of "I" in *Walden* reports the total to be 1,811.

Page 176 . . . . *"When a historian allows . . . ."* John Leonard Clive, *Not by Fact Alone* (London: Collins Harvill, 1990). Quotation from pp. 32–33.

Page 177. *Insofar as I can tell, ...*

The code of medical ethics known as Maimonides's Oath reflects this understanding beautifully. In part, it reads, "Grant me the strength, time, and opportunity always to correct the knowledge I have acquired, always to extend its domain. For [the unknown truth] is immense . . . ."

A Hedge Against Preoccupation

Page 178. *"Peripheral vision."* Alan Watts, *The Way of Zen* (New York: Knopf Doubleday Publishing Group, 2011). Quotation from p. 15.

Page 179. *"The curse of Hitler . . . ."* Winston Churchill, "War of the Unknown Warriors" (speech), London. July 1940.

Page 183. *Like the (quite possibly apocryphal) poor spider . . . .*

Also, when we rigidly, robotically, behave in plan-executing mode, we neglect events *within* ourselves. I suspect, for instance, that digestive issues I have had throughout my life go back to my cooperation in my parents' daily "plan" that I finish every bit of food on the plate they set before me at meals. At a thousand unrecorded points in time, I was asked, "Are you going to finish all those carrots and roasted potatoes before you watch TV?," and I grunted dutifully "Uhuh" and chowed them down, thoughtless of internal consequences. Now, to remind myself to eat in closer sync with my true appetite—and in closer sync with real effects on my GI tract—I take measures that required decades for me to devise or learn about. For one thing, I now cut a big sandwich into halves, then cut one of those halves into halves. At each cut in the sandwich—essentially the halfway mark and the three-quarter mark—I chew and consider whether to go on or to save what's left for later. By that means, I've become more present to my food and feel better.

TOLERATING AMBIGUITY

Page 186. *"An arrogant twit."* Gene Weingarten and Michael E. Ruane, "Maya Angelou Says King Memorial Inscription Makes Him Look 'Arrogant,'" *The Washington Post*, August 30, 2011.

Page 187. *"Selfishly."* Mark 10:35.

Page 187. *"Before we condemn them . . . ."* Martin Luther King, Jr., "The Drum Major Instinct" (speech), February 1968.

Page 188. *"Truth and beauty . . . ."* Mark Singer, "The Man Who Forgets Nothing," *The New Yorker*, March 19, 2020.

Page 189. *"The object of life . . . ."* William Empson, *Seven Types of Ambiguity* (Cambridge, MA: New Directions, 1966). Quotation from p. 247.

Page 190. *"There's no God . . . ."* Lewis White Beck, *Six Secular Philosophers* (London: Thoemmes Press, 1997). Quotation from p. 113.

Page 190. *Or take two lines.* Jon Kabat-Zinn, *Wherever You Go, There You Are* (New York: Hachette Books, 1994). Quotation from p. 135.

Page 190. *"Furious, and wild . . . ."* Nicholas Kilmer, *A Place in Normandy* (New York: Henry Holt and Co., 1997). Quotation from p. 243.

Page 191. *"Life is much more . . . ."* F. Scott Fitzgerald, *The Great Gatsby* (New York: Charles Scribner's Sons, 1925). Quotation from p. 4.

Page 191. *"The test of a . . . ."* F. Scott Fitzgerald, *The Crack-Up*, ed. Edmund Wilson (New York: New Directions Books, 1945). Quotation from p. 69.

OUR DYING

Page 195. *"What does it mean . . . ."* Ernest Becker, *The Denial of Death* (New York: Free Press, 2007). Quotation from p. 87.

Page 195. *"Humankind cannot bear very . . . ."* T. S. Eliot, *The Four Quartets* (Boston: HMH Books, 2014). Quotation from p. 40.

Page 196. *"I have read that . . . ."* Robert Hendrickson, *The Literary Life and Other Curiosities* (New York: Viking, 1981).

Page 198. *". . . Consonants slipping into drifts."* George Ellenbogen, *The Rhino Gate Poems* (Quebec: Signal Editions, 1996). Quotation from p. 47.

Could our second president, John Adams—someone famous for his passion for right order—have been preparing, in old age, for his own dissolution when he imagined punctuation marks floating free in space, out of all relation to the verbal projects of a human being? Here's an excerpt from a late Adams letter quoted by biographer David McCullough:

> I never delighted much in contemplating commas and colons . . . but now . . . if I attempt to look at these little objects, I find my imagination . . . roaming in the Milky Way, among the nebulae, those mighty orbs . . . which compose the incomprehensible universe . . . .
>
> — SOURCE: *JOHN ADAMS*, BY DAVID McCULLOUGH, P. 630

Page 199. "*So long lives this . . . .*" William Shakespeare, *Shakespeare's Sonnets* (Boston: Ticknor and Fields, 1832). Quotation from p. 24.

CODA: THE COMEDIENNE OF GRAMMAR

Page 203. "*Never place a period . . . .*" Used in the "God Is Still Speaking" campaign of the United Church of Christ.

Index

Acknowledgments

As my reader may recall, this book opens with a real (nighttime) dream of mine set outside the door to a kitchen—that same kitchen where, if you believe the dream, this book was prepared, like soup.

If my dreaming eye had gone right past that door and into the kitchen while my culinary efforts were still in progress there, it would have beheld a teeming throng of wordy sous chefs. A number would be crowding 'round the oversized pot I used, adding new ingredients to mine or astutely seasoning it all. Others would be standing back a few short feet, making terse pronouncements such as "That's just not enough" or "What?! Too much!"

The final product, which you've been consuming, is in good part theirs. I hope that the list that follows leaves none of them out, since I'm indebted to them all. They are:

Yusef Abdolmohammadi	Carolyn Bond
Victoria Barrett	Janet Buchwald
Nicole Belmonte	Sarah Buermann
Chris Beneke	Jayne and Leon Cantor
Joan and Ethan Bolker	John Case

Dave Colozzi	Christine Kraft
Wiley Davi	Rabbi Lawrence Kushner
Karen Delorey	John Lanza
Jackie Donnelly	Kathy Leydon-Conway
George Ellenbogen	Tracy Marks
Greg Farber	Linda McJannet
Evelyn Farbman	Brad McKenna
De Ann Finkel	Sally Millichamp
Tom Finn	Ray Mosher
Scott Fivelson	Ann Munson
Jim Foritano	Richard Paseman
Wayne Goins	Sheila Reindl
Joan Goldmann	Lynne Reveno
Kent Greenawalt	Rachele Ros-Kessel
Richard Griffin	Rob Ross
Susan Haverson	David and Elly Rubin
Jim Hornfischer	Bob Schueler
Justin Hoskins	Nick Schupbach
Paul Hughes	Elizabeth Segal
Martha Keating	Lynn Senne
Diane Kellogg	Bob Sprich
Nick and Julia Kilmer	Kathleen Sullivan
David Klingsberg	Judith Taplitz

and, not least, my loyal daughter and son,
Rachel and Noam Weinstein.

Other names that need recording here, with thanks, are those of folks involved in designing this book, checking every detail about it with care, and marketing it. I have in mind especially Janica Smith, Ayman Alalao, Marie Stirk, Joy Xiang, Lynette Smith, Heidi Eliason, Stephanie Chandler, and, most recently, Connie Tang.

Most of the book's illustrations—including its cover illustration—are the fine work of Juliana Duclos.

All that having been said, special mention is required in the cases of five people.

My brother Warren's commentary on the first draft of this book was so long and thoughtful, it was practically a book in its own right.

Cath Gulick may have been the best editor I've worked with in my life. It's a near toss-up between her and Sharron Dorr, the editor of the original version of this book.

Always a booster of my writing, my late wife, Diane Weinstein, read and responded wisely to every iteration of the original version—occasionally giving me the very words I was looking for. In addition, Diane synthesized the many responses of others to my drafts, tracked down sources for me, brainstormed with me for a title, compiled the book's index.... There was no aspect of the book untouched by her loving influence.

My love and soulmate of later years, Suzanne Hoffman, flatly refused to let me drop my plans for this book when my original publisher, Quest Books, closed its doors after half a century in business. Her belief in me has bordered on the irrational at times, but I don't seem to have objected strongly enough to disabuse her of it. It and our feelings for each other have been sustaining me.

Last of all, I thank Quest Books for cordially returning to me all my rights to the original, shorter and much different version of this book, whose title was *Grammar for the Soul.*

I'm one lucky, grateful man.

— LW

About the Author

From 1973 to 1983, Lawrence Weinstein taught writing at Harvard University, where he cofounded Harvard's Writing Center. He then joined the English Department of Bentley University, where he became Director of Bentley's Expository Writing Program. His books include *Writing at the Threshold*, a bestseller of the National Council of Teachers of English, and *Money Changes Everything*.

Two of Weinstein's full-length plays have received professional productions. One, *The La Vidas' Landlord*, has been optioned for Broadway production.

He welcomes comments on this book via email, at lweinstein@bentley.edu.

/

Made in the USA
Las Vegas, NV
01 August 2021

27092746R00152